In a world of higl

WHEN FASHION *turns* DEADLY

A Falcon Point Suspense

TRACI HUNTER ABRAMSON
& SIAN ANN BESSEY

Covenant Communications, Inc.

Cover image: Created with AI, *Portrait of a Stunning Woman with Flowing Auburn Hair and Piercing Green Eyes against a Rich Garnet-Colored Backdrop* © CandyAI, Adobe Stock; *Eiffel Tower at Night* © Sian Ann Bessey and Traci Hunter Abramson

Cover design by Christina Marcano © 2024 by Covenant Communications, Inc.

Published by Covenant Communications, Inc.
American Fork, Utah

Copyright © 2024 by Traci Hunter Abramson and Sian Ann Bessey
All rights reserved. No part of this book may be reproduced in any format or in any medium without the written permission of the publisher, Covenant Communications, Inc., PO Box 416, American Fork, UT 84003. The views expressed within this work are the sole responsibility of the authors and do not necessarily reflect the position of Covenant Communications, Inc., or any other entity.

This is a work of fiction. The characters, names, incidents, places, and dialogue are either products of the authors' imaginations, and are not to be construed as real, or are used fictitiously.

Library of Congress Cataloging-in-Publication Data

Name: Traci Hunter Abramson and Sian Ann Bessey
Title: When Fashion Turns Deadly / Traci Hunter Abramson and Sian Ann Bessey
Description: American Fork, UT : Covenant Communications, Inc. [2024]
Identifiers: Library of Congress Control Number 2024934740 | ISBN: 978-1-52442-713-9
LC record available at https://lccn.loc.gov/2024934740

Printed in the United States of America
First Printing: November 2024

30 29 28 27 26 25 24   10 9 8 7 6 5 4 3 2 1

UNCLASSIFIED disclaimer: All statements of fact, opinion, or analysis expressed are those of the authors and do not reflect the official positions or views of the US Government. Nothing in the contents should be construed as asserting or implying US Government authentication of information or endorsement of the authors' views.

To Samantha Millburn,
our remarkable editor and cherished friend

ACKNOWLEDGMENTS

Although two names appear on the cover of this book, there are many others who played a significant role in its production. We are especially grateful to our editor, Samantha Millburn (she truly is as amazing as she sounds), and the rest of the Covenant family, especially Christina Marcano, Shara Meredith, Ashlyn LaOrange, and Brookelyn Jones.

Thank you, Sarah Eden, for allowing us to tag along on your research trip to Paris. This book would not be what it is today without our visit to the Conciergerie, our impromptu hike to Sacré Cœur, and our evening stroll beneath the Eiffel Tower. Thanks also to Andrea Steele and Dianne Hunter for answering our many questions about the world of fashion and modeling, and to Mandy Biesinger, Sarah Olsen, and Lara Abramson for your feedback on the early drafts of this novel.

We appreciate the support of our families and the efforts of the CIA Publication Classification Review Board in helping us make our writing deadlines. And we are especially grateful to our readers who love our Falcon Point characters and have encouraged us to continue their adventures.

CHAPTER 1

Marit shifted the plum-colored velvet cushion at her back, adjusted her position in the gray-tweed wingback armchair, and recrossed her ankles. Elegance. Grace. It was what her agent, Esmee, demanded of all her models, particularly when they were meeting with clothing designers. And today, it wasn't just any designer; it was Ralph Molenaar, the Netherlands' foremost authority on fashion and the man whose designs were causing the biggest buzz at this year's Paris Fashion Week.

"Sorry to keep you waiting, ladies." Ralph walked in wearing a black turtleneck and black trousers. His assistant, Adriana, was only a couple of steps behind, carrying a sheaf of papers. "Casting went longer than I'd anticipated."

He hardly needed to tell them that. Esmee had had at least thirty models standing in line for casting today. Marit was grateful that she and her colleague Nadia had been spared the torturously long wait. Several weeks ago, Ralph had requested that they both work his show. For Esmee, his singling out two of her models was a huge feather in her cap. For Marit, the personal invitation was a dream come true.

"I don't think those lines are getting shorter any time soon," Esmee said as she, Marit, and Nadia rose to their feet to greet him.

Ralph gave a rueful smile. "A designer's only as good as his next season's designs, Esmee. You know that better than anyone."

"Yes, well, if the pieces Marit and Nadia tried on earlier today are any indication, you have nothing to worry about for a while."

This time, his smile was genuine. "You liked them, huh?"

"They're magnificent," Esmee said.

He reached for the papers in Adriana's hands and rifled through them. "So, you've already had your fittings?"

"Yes," Marit said. "We're ready."

"Excellent." He marked something on his papers. "I'm glad you're both here. It's good to work with models I know."

Marit smiled. The feeling was mutual. She was always more at ease working for someone familiar, because every clothing collection was different, and it helped when she knew how the designer liked to run his or her show. She was quite sure Nadia felt the same. The two of them had modeled together more often than not, which wasn't necessarily surprising since they were both Dutch, worked through the same agency, and had contrasting appearances that gave designers like Ralph a chance to showcase a variety of colors to their best advantage. Marit's long blonde hair and fair skin was a perfect foil for Nadia's short, tight black curls and darker complexion.

"Do you have any particular concerns?" Marit asked.

"Coster is supplying us with jewelry," he said. "I've approved each piece, and there isn't a single one that's not eye-catching. As much as I appreciate the opportunity to feature Dutch gems in my show, your job is to make sure the buyers are more interested in the clothing than the accessories."

Marit could not prevent the excitement that rose within her at the reminder. Her boyfriend, Lars, was Coster Diamonds' official photographer, and he was coming to Paris with the jewelry, which meant they'd have almost two whole weeks together in the city. Even though they'd both be working, she could hardly wait for him to arrive.

"We can do that," Nadia said, bringing Marit's attention back to Ralph's request. "Your designs don't need bling to set them apart."

Nadia was right. Ralph's lack of sparkles or ornamentation was one of the things that made his designs so universally popular.

Even his office reflected his style: classic lines, subdued tones, with a few strategically placed accent colors. His large desk was uncluttered, and the lone decorations in the room were the half dozen framed award certificates and an oil painting of Dutch tulip fields hanging on the wall. The only thing that glittered in the entire room was the light gleaming off the metallic trim on the closet door's keypad lock.

"Well then, I don't think we have anything else to discuss." He handed the papers back to Adriana.

"Thank you, Ralph." Esmee reached for her coat and put it on.

Marit and Nadia did the same. Then, lifting her shoulder bag from the floor, Marit pulled out her red beanie. Late February in Paris was chilly, especially in the evenings, after the sun went down.

Waiting for the women to precede him out of the office, Ralph locked the door behind them.

"Ralph!"

They all turned. A man with tousled brown hair was standing with one hand on the doorframe of an office down the hall.

"Maggie needs you to sign off on something right away," he called.

"And so the pre-Fashion Week emergencies begin," Ralph said. "If you will excuse me, ladies." He inclined his head toward them. "Marit and Nadia, I'll see you both backstage. Esmee, always a pleasure." He headed down the hall at a brisk walk.

The three women went the other way, toward the lift.

Unfortunately, their departure was poorly timed. It seemed that almost everyone in the building was leaving work for the day. The lift stopped at each of the five floors on their way down from Ralph and his team's floor, and by the time they reached the lobby, Marit was more than ready to exit the confined space. She, Esmee, and Nadia joined the general exodus toward the outer doors, and as she walked, Marit opened her bag to retrieve her gloves—but found only one. With a sinking heart, she rooted through her bag again.

"Hang on," she said. "I've lost a glove."

Nadia frowned. "We don't have that far to walk to the Metro station. You can just put your hands in your pockets."

"I could, but I really don't want to lose my gloves." Marit wasn't going to take the time to explain to Nadia that Lars had given them to her for Christmas and—quite apart from the fact that they were her favorite pair—he'd notice right away if she stopped using them.

"When was the last time you wore them?" Esmee asked.

"On my way here." Marit closed her bag with a frustrated sigh. "It must have dropped out of my bag in Ralph's office when I grabbed my hat." With resignation, she eyed the congestion around the lift. "It's going to take a while to get back to the sixth floor. You two don't need to wait. I'll go up and see if Ralph will let me into the office again, and then I'll meet you back at the flat afterward."

"Okay." Nadia didn't hesitate. Marit could hardly blame her. She was probably as anxious as Marit was to take off her high heels and put on some slippers.

"You know the Metro stop you need?" Esmee asked.

"Madeleine," Marit said.

Esmee nodded. "All right. We'll see you soon."

Moving against the flow of people, Marit made her way back to the lift. The wait seemed interminable, and when the doors finally opened, another flood of people exited. She waited until the lift was empty, walked in, and pushed the button for the sixth floor. The lift went up one floor and stopped. The doors opened to a cluster of office employees, each anxious to go home.

"It's going up," Marit said in French.

Ignoring the grumbles, she pushed the door closed and prepared herself to repeat the same warning four more times.

By the time she reached the sixth floor, the receptionist's chair was empty and the lights in the foyer were dimmed. Hurrying toward Ralph's office, she scanned the hall for a chink of light beneath a door. Fashion Week—with all its crazy, last-minute madness—began next Monday. Even if Ralph had resolved Maggie's pressing issue and they'd both managed to leave in the last twenty minutes, there had to be someone working late tonight.

She strained her ears. There were voices coming from somewhere. The end of the hall, maybe? She continued past three closed doors and had reached Ralph's office when she heard the hum and click of an electronic lock. She frowned. It had sounded as though it had come from inside Ralph's office, but no light showed beneath the door. Seconds later, the door handle shifted. Startled, Marit stepped back three paces. The door opened, and the man who'd called out to Ralph earlier appeared. He was wearing a jacket and gloves, and his unruly hair was covered by a navy knit hat. A canvas messenger bag was slung over his shoulder, and in his hand, he held a phone.

The moment he saw Marit, his jaw tightened. "What are you doing here? Ralph's gone."

"I think I dropped my glove in his office." When the man didn't immediately invite her in, she continued. "I was hoping to check to see if it's under the chair where I was sitting."

He glanced up and down the hall. "Be quick," he said, flipping on the light and finally stepping aside so she could enter. "I had to drop something off for Ralph, but he doesn't like anyone in here when he's not around."

Marit wasted no time. She crossed to the armchair where she'd been sitting, and a wave of relief washed over her. Her missing glove was lying in plain sight, right beside the plum-colored cushion.

"Got it!" she said, raising it so he could see. "Thanks so much for letting me in."

He gave a curt nod, his attention on the hallway rather than on her. "Come on, then. I need to get going."

Marit stepped into the hall, but not before noticing that Ralph's desk was as clear of papers now as it had been earlier. Whatever the man had delivered had not been left on the desk. She glanced at the closet door keypad reflecting back the overhead light. Perhaps that was the lock she'd heard from the hall. He must have put something in there instead.

Keeping his back to her, the man pulled the door shut and tugged on the handle to make sure it was locked. Satisfied, he hiked the strap of his messenger bag a little higher on his shoulder. A ping sounded, announcing the arrival of the lift. Marit turned toward the lobby in time to see the lift doors open. A man dressed in a custodian's uniform stepped out, dragging a cart behind him.

"If we hurry, we might be able to catch the lift," she said, starting down the hall.

The man didn't reply. She turned her head to repeat herself, but he had disappeared. Puzzled, she studied the empty hall. Either he'd slipped into another room, or one of those doors led to a staircase. No matter which it was, he obviously wasn't interested in catching the lift. The lift doors thudded closed, and she stifled a groan. Her hesitation had cost her. Goodness only knew how long she'd have to wait until it came back up. She'd just have to hope that the custodian now emptying the bins in the foyer was a little friendlier than the other man had been.

CHAPTER 2

Cole stood in the dark electrical access closet and pressed the button on his watch to illuminate the time. Any minute, the guard should pass by and take the elevator to the next floor down. Cole had already spent two nights hiding in here to time his approach and set up a visual override of the security cameras in the hallway.

Cole's boss at the CIA had lent him to the Brussels field office specifically to break through the defenses of Lamar Peeters's headquarters and infiltrate his private office.

Interpol and the CIA both suspected Peeters himself had been involved in the theft of the designs of a new military drone, a theft that had occurred only last week. If their sources were correct, Peeters intended to sell the designs to the highest bidder in a matter of days.

The mere thought of such advanced weaponry falling into the wrong hands sent a shudder through Cole. Ready or not, tonight he had to make his move and recover those schematics.

Footsteps sounded in the hall. Cole counted off the seconds to when the guard would reach the elevator. The elevator dinged.

Cole waited for the hum of the doors opening and closing before he engaged the override on the cameras. Then he pressed his watch again, this time engaging the timer. Ninety seconds until the laser sensors would activate. Thirty-nine minutes to break into Peeters's office and get back out of sight.

Cole opened the door and sprinted down the hall. He reached the cipher lock and held a code override device to the scanner at the top. Seconds ticked by, the display on the device flashing numbers with ridiculous speed. Thirty seconds left. Maybe less. His heartbeat quickened. Stay and hope the six-digit code cleared in time, or run back to the closet and try again after the next guard pass?

The fifth number clicked into place. One more.

Cole remained in the hall. Fifteen seconds left. Ten. Five.

The last number illuminated his screen, and Cole quickly typed it onto the keypad with his gloved hand. The lock clicked back. He opened the door and quickly slipped inside, closing the door silently behind him.

A sigh of relief escaped him. First obstacle down.

Cole pulled out his night-vision scope and looked through it to verify that Peeters didn't have any laser sensors in his office. Once satisfied, Cole crossed to the desk. No laptop. He opened the top desk drawer easily, finding notepads and pens neatly arranged inside. He pulled on the second one, but it was locked.

The metal key lock took only a few seconds to pick, but when Cole opened the drawer, he discovered a new challenge. The entire inside of the drawer had been fitted with a custom safe, only this time Cole had to work through an old-fashioned tumbler system rather than a digital keypad.

"Great," he muttered under his breath.

Too bad his girlfriend wasn't here. With her years of working undercover at a bank in Austria, Isabelle was a pro at this. He knew he could get the job done, but he would have preferred facing this type of lock with a bit more time to spare or with Isabelle at his side.

He pulled his listening device from his coat pocket and attached the three receivers to the left side. Then he slipped the earbuds into his ears.

Slowly, he turned the dial one number at a time. Nine minutes later, he reached the first: twenty-two. He started back in the other direction. Another ten minutes. Eighty-seven.

His palms sweating inside his gloves, he slowly turned the dial to the right again. Twelve minutes left. He clicked past the final number: sixteen. Frustrated that he had gone too far, he spun the dial several times and went through the combination again before turning the dial back to zero. He pulled on the handle and opened the safe.

Relieved to finally be in, he peered at the contents: a laptop, three rolled documents secured with rubber bands, a pistol, several stacks of hundred-euro bills, and a manila file folder at the bottom. Cole took everything but the pistol and the money. Once it was all secured in his backpack, he started to close the safe, then reconsidered. No thief would leave the money, and Cole needed this to look like a robbery.

He grabbed the stacks of cash and stuffed them into his backpack. Then he secured the safe, locked the top drawer, and checked the time. Two minutes left.

Ensuring he left the desk as he found it, sans the contents of the safe, Cole rushed to the door.

He counted off the seconds. Then with a silent prayer, he opened the door, did a quick scan to ensure the lasers were turned off, and sprinted back to the closet. He shut the door behind him as the elevator doors chimed. Cole grabbed the connection to the security override and pulled it free.

His breath rushed out of him. That was close.

He leaned against the wall and willed his heart to settle. Another four hours until the offices would open for the day and the guards would change. Until then, he had nothing to do but remain invisible and silent.

After twelve straight hours of casting calls, Marit was more than ready to be off her feet. If every designer let her cut through red tape the way Ralph had yesterday, the week leading up to Paris's fashion shows wouldn't be half so exhausting. Rolling her shoulders, she unlocked the door to the agency flat she shared with Nadia and walked in.

Moments later, her phone rang. A quick glance at the name on the screen put a smile on her face. "Hi, Lars!"

"Hey, am I catching you at a good time?"

"Yes. I just arrived back at the flat." She set her bag on the counter. "How's the inventory going?" Lars was still in Amsterdam, preparing the Coster jewelry for transportation to Paris.

"I just finished," he said. "And now that I have a better idea of how much the contents of these cases are worth, I'm doubly glad I'm in charge of recording images of each piece, not safeguarding them once they leave here."

"I think you'll get some great shots of the jewelry on the models at the shows."

"I'm sure I will," he said. "I only wish I were heading to Paris today."

"Me too." Three more days. It shouldn't seem like a long time, but it did.

Lars must have been feeling the same way, because he sighed. "I miss you."

"I miss you too." A knock sounded at the door. Puzzled, Marit glanced at it. "Hey, Lars, someone's at the door, and Nadia isn't here right now. I'd better go see who it is. Can I call you later?"

"Sure," he said. "I'll be working late tonight. If I don't answer right away, I'll call you back."

"Sounds good. Thanks." Disconnecting the call, she set her phone on the counter next to her purse and crossed the short distance to the door. She pulled it open. Two uniformed police officers stood outside. "*Bonsoir*," she said, automatically switching to French.

"Marit Jansen?" the taller of the two men asked.

"Yes." Marit's grasp on the doorknob tightened. How did they know her name? More to the point, *why* did they know her name?

"My name is Capitaine Dupont." He gestured toward his colleague. "This is Brigadier Blanchet. We're conducting an official investigation of a recent incident and believe you can help shed some light on it for us."

Marit's thoughts immediately flew to her involvement in helping to apprehend drug smugglers in Amsterdam almost two months before. But there could not possibly be a connection between that episode and these officers. Cole had assured Isabelle, Lars, and her that the authorities had the final phase of that investigation well in hand. Besides, even if they'd discovered another loose thread, why would the local French police be involved?

"I doubt that I can be of any help to you," she said. "I don't even know what you're investigating."

Capitaine Dupont inclined his head as though conceding the point. "That can be remedied. If you will come with us, we shall go over things in more detail at the police station."

Marit stared at them, the first hint of fear stealing into her heart. "You want me to come with you now? For questioning?"

"Yes, mademoiselle."

She looked from the capitaine's stern expression to the brigadier's. Neither gave anything away. Her fingers ached from their grip on the doorknob, a sure sign that she was not dreaming. "What's this all about?"

"As I said, mademoiselle, we shall discuss it further at the station."

Marit battled her racing thoughts. What was she to do? She had no experience with police interrogations. She didn't even know her legal rights in France. Would they let her call someone? Or at least text Esmee or Nadia before forcing her to go with them?

"I must let someone know where I'm going," she said. "My friends will worry about me if I'm gone for long."

"One phone call," Capitaine Dupont said. "I see you already have your coat on. If you wish to bring your handbag, you may do that. You'll need nothing more."

Attempting to think through the fog of shock, Marit backed into the room. The police officers stayed in the doorway, watching. She slipped the handles of her bag over her shoulder and reached for her phone. Who should she call?

Realistically, it was doubtful that Esmee would miss her until tomorrow. Her agent would only start panicking if Marit didn't show up for her final fitting with Kyle Adams. Nadia would probably assume that she was out with others this evening and would think nothing of going to bed before Marit arrived back. Lars was too far away to do anything but worry if she told him what she was facing. The same could be said for her parents. Her fingers hovered over the names in her favorites list. As far as she knew, there was only one person who might have the contacts and experience necessary to help her out of this situation.

She pressed Cole's number and put the phone to her ear. "Please pick up, Cole," she whispered. "Please pick up."

The phone rang five times before rolling into Cole's voice mail. Swallowing her disappointment, she turned her back on the police officers and spoke into the phone in English.

"Cole, this is Marit. I'm in Paris for Fashion Week, staying in an agency flat on Place de la Madeleine. Two police officers just arrived at my door and claim they need to take me in for questioning. I have no idea what it's about, but the vibe they're giving off tells me it's serious. I don't know if they'll let me make a phone call once I'm at the police station, but if you get this message soon, I could use your advice."

"It's time to go, mademoiselle." Capitaine Dupont's tone barely hid his impatience.

Marit disconnected her call and tucked her phone into her pocket. Grabbing her flat keys from the counter, she walked to the door. She may not know what this was about, but she knew she had nothing to hide. Her trembling fingers notwithstanding, that fact alone was enough to keep her chin up. "All right," she said. "I'm ready."

CHAPTER 3

Cole stepped aboard the train that would take him on his first leg to Vienna, a duffel bag in one hand and his backpack in the other. Though he wasn't thrilled with the two transfers and the twelve hours it would take him to get home, it beat trying to cut through the red tape required for him to transport his firearms through airport security. After so many years living in Europe, Cole was well versed in how to bypass that problem at the local train stations.

Cole made his way to his seat and settled his backpack beneath the chair in front of him. No way was he letting his extra ammo out of his sight.

He pulled his cell phone from his pocket to see who had called when he'd been boarding the train. A voice mail from Marit? Why would she be calling him? Probably trying to plan a surprise for Lars's birthday.

Curious, Cole hit the Play button and lifted the phone to his ear. Marit's voice trembled when she explained that the police were taking her in for questioning. That couldn't be right.

Cole played the message again. He shook his head. Whether he wanted to or not, it looked like he was making an unexpected detour through Paris.

Grateful that the train hadn't left yet, he gathered his bags, left the train, and pulled up the Omio app on his phone. After a quick search of train options from Brussels to Paris, he bought a new ticket. Too bad he hadn't gotten her message a little sooner. If he had, he might have made the train that had departed only three minutes ago. As it was, he'd have to wait another half hour for the next one.

He looked up the platform number and headed for his ride. What in the world had Marit gotten herself involved in?

Bypassing a family of five who were blocking the majority of the platform, he dialed Marit's number, not surprised when the call went unanswered. Most likely, the police had already taken possession of her phone. With Marit not answering, he dialed Lars. He also didn't answer.

Knowing his cousin, the man was probably desperately trying to get to Paris to find some answers of his own.

Cole pulled up the address for the place where Marit was staying and searched for the police department closest to her. He copied the address into the notes app on his phone. With any luck, he would be there within two hours. If she was a suspect in a crime, it was highly possible he would arrive before they tried to interrogate her. If she was simply a witness, he could make sure she was safe before he returned to Vienna.

He reached the correct platform and passed the crowd of passengers already gathered there until he reached the far end, where he could make a phone call with some level of privacy.

He dialed Isabelle's number.

"Hey there. Are you back?" she asked in lieu of a greeting.

"No." Cole switched from English to German in case the French couple nearby cared about his conversation. The likelihood of them speaking German was marginally lower than their being fluent in English. "Marit left me a message. She was taken in by the police for questioning."

Concern filled Isabelle's voice when she responded, also speaking in German. "For what?"

"I don't know. I'm not sure she knows either." He pushed aside his regret that he wouldn't be able to see Isabelle as soon as he'd planned. "I'm taking the train to Paris to find out what's going on."

"Let me know if you want me to meet you there. I can always take a long weekend."

"Thanks." A long weekend in Paris with Isabelle. The prospect had definite possibilities, assuming his boss would let him have the time off. "I'll give you a call as soon as I know anything."

"One more thing," Isabelle said.

"Yeah?"

"Does Jasmine know you're diverting?" she asked, referring to the CIA station chief in Vienna.

"Not yet." Cole glanced at the other passengers wandering toward him. "Any chance you want to let her know what's going on?"

"Not a lot of privacy at the train station, huh?"

Appreciating her perception, he nodded even though she couldn't see him. "Exactly."

"I'll call Jasmine, and I'll see if she has any contacts with the Paris police who can help us find out why Marit was taken in."

"Thanks. I appreciate it."

"No problem. Travel safe."

"I will. I miss you." The words rolled off his tongue with such ease, he could barely believe they'd been seriously dating for only four months.

"I miss you too."

His mood lighter after talking to Isabelle, Cole ended the call. What a difference a few months could make. When they had first started dating, he had completely let things slide between them when he'd gone out on missions. Now she was the first person he thought of when his itinerary changed. This was getting weird, but he had to admit, he rather liked knowing she was waiting for his call.

The train pulled up to the platform, and Cole boarded. He found his assigned seat, stored his duffel in the overhead compartment, and pulled his secure laptop out of his backpack. Time to do some research on recent crimes in Paris.

Marit had no idea how long she'd been sitting alone in the interrogation room. The police officer behind the desk at the station had taken possession of her phone and bag when she'd first arrived. Without a clock on the wall, it was impossible to know for sure. But if the gnawing of her stomach and the ache in her back from sitting on a hard chair for too long was any indication, a significant amount of time had passed.

At first, she'd sat quietly, desperately trying to think of anything she might have seen that would place her on the police's radar. She'd come up empty. Pacing the room while reflecting on the happenings at every place she'd visited since arriving in Paris had delivered no better results. Until someone told her why she was being held for questioning, she was completely in the dark. And she was rapidly discovering that she did not like that state at all.

Smoothing her shaking hands across her knees, she kept her eyes on the door. At her right, a wall of mirrors looked down on her. She had no way of knowing how many officers were watching her from the other side, but like a chill gradually creeping up her spine, she felt their cool appraisal. The remaining walls were white, the floor a gray linoleum. The only furniture was the black plastic chair she was using, the small table before her, and the orange plastic chair on the other side of the table.

She released an unsteady breath. It shouldn't bother her that the chairs didn't match. It was a trivial thing. But it was easier to focus on the lack of aesthetics in the room than on the lack of another person. And orange chairs were, by definition, unpleasant. Almost as unpleasant as being forced to wait for her interrogation to begin.

Her thoughts shifted to Lars. Had he wondered why she hadn't called him back yet? Had he tried to call her? And Cole? She had no way of knowing if he'd listened to her voice message or what he could do to help her now that she no longer had her phone. But she drew some comfort from believing that he would do *something*—even if it was only to let Lars know what had happened. It went against Cole's basic nature to do nothing.

She closed her eyes, trying to imagine herself anywhere else. And then she heard the door handle move. Opening her eyes, she watched in silence as the door swung wide and Capitaine Dupont entered.

"I apologize for keeping you waiting," he said, taking a seat on the orange chair.

Marit seriously doubted he was the slightest bit sorry, but she thought it best to refrain from sharing the thought. The length of time they planned to keep her in this awful room was very likely correlated to her agreeability.

"I'm still waiting to be told why I'm here," she said.

"When did you arrive in Paris?" he asked, completely ignoring her comment.

"Three days ago," she said. "I came in by train from Amsterdam with my agent, Esmee Scheffer, and a few others from her modeling agency. We're here for Fashion Week."

"What did you do yesterday?"

Yesterday. Marit mentally sifted through her day's schedule. "I ate breakfast at the flat and then took the Metro for casting at Dior. After I received my callback time for today, I went for my initial fitting with Ralph Molenaar's team. I was there until the end of the workday. Then I returned to the flat and didn't leave again all evening."

"Was anyone with you?" he asked.

"Yes. My agent, Esmee, and my colleague Nadia."

"All day?" he pressed.

"Yes. Nadia and I are sharing the flat, and we had the same appointments."

He eyed her sternly. "Then why do we have an eyewitness who claims you were alone in the vicinity of Ralph Molenaar's office in the early evening?"

Memory flooded back. "Esmee, Nadia, and I were in Ralph's office together. Right after we left, Ralph was called into another office. It was only after Esmee,

Nadia, and I took the lift to the lobby that I discovered I left one of my gloves in Ralph's office. I went back up by myself to find it."

"And did you find it?" The look in his eyes suggested that he didn't believe she owned a pair of gloves, let alone had lost one of them.

"I did."

"Where?"

"In Ralph's office."

"According to Monsieur Molenaar, he did not return to his office after his visit with you and your colleagues. How did you get in?"

"A man—one of Ralph's employees—was already in the room. He waited for me to retrieve it before leaving."

The capitaine set his elbows on the table and leaned forward. "Describe this man."

"Twenty-two to twenty-three years old," Marit said. "Between one point eight two and one point eight five meters tall, and about eighty kilograms. Curly brown hair grown out of his original haircut, brown eyes, pitted complexion. He was wearing Ralph Molenaar jeans and a cheap black T-shirt with a picture of a hamburger and fries on it. He spoke Dutch but had a slight accent. I doubt that it's his first language."

Capitaine Dupont stared at her. "You seem very sure of these details."

"I'm a professional model, Capitaine. I notice such things as clothing and brands."

"And height and weight?"

"Yes," she said simply. "Those things too."

He took a moment to consider his next question. "Tell me about your interaction with this man."

"I heard him before I saw him," Marit said, and then she proceeded to recount her interaction with Ralph's employee from the time he opened the door to Ralph's office to the time he disappeared from sight.

The capitaine listened intently, and when she finished, he appeared thoughtful. "And did you see or hear anyone else while you were there?"

"I thought I heard voices farther down the hall, but I didn't see anyone there. Other than those using the lift, the only other person I saw was the custodian, who arrived as I was leaving."

"Can you describe the custodian?" he asked.

Marit took a deep breath. "Late fifties, gray, thinning hair, and black-rimmed glasses. He was about one point seven seven meters tall and weighed about ninety kilograms. He wore a pale-blue jumpsuit with a red-and-white *Pierre's Cleaners* logo on the upper left pocket and had his ID hanging on a lanyard around his neck."

"I'm impressed, mademoiselle. Few people remember such details so well. It's a shame you didn't also notice the name on the tag."

"Tomas Moulin," she said.

His eyes widened slightly, and he inclined his head. "I'm doubly impressed."

"To be honest, Capitaine Dupont, I'd rather have you allow me to leave than have you be impressed by my ability to recall details. You still haven't told me why I'm here."

He leaned back in his chair and eyed her thoughtfully. "We are investigating a theft," he said.

This time it was Marit's eyes that widened. "At Ralph's offices?"

He offered her a half smile. "Yes. But that is all I am willing to share at this point in the investigation. And I must ask for your discretion in not discussing this with anyone else." He rose. "If you will follow me, Brigadier Blanchet will take down your contact information, and then you are free to go."

Marit stood, relief causing her voice to catch. "I can leave?"

"Yes, mademoiselle." He turned toward the door. "This way."

CHAPTER 4

Isabelle sat on the chair beside the living room window, an afghan draped over her legs to ward off the chill in the room, a book open on her lap, and her cell phone lying idly on the armrest. She ignored the book and stared at the dark screen on her cell. Why hadn't Cole texted?

He'd messaged her three hours ago, after he'd boarded the train for Paris. That trip took only an hour and twenty-two minutes. She'd checked. Whether Cole opted for a cab or public transit, he should have arrived at the police station over an hour ago.

The pressure of not knowing built up in her lungs and escaped in a sigh. She hated being in the dark.

Tossing the book and the afghan aside, Isabelle rose to her feet and crossed to the window. Her CIA training kicked in, and she did a quick analysis of the street below. Pedestrians heading toward the train, a man scraping ice off his windshield. When she determined nothing was amiss, she returned to her chair.

On the surface, her life was exactly what her former classmates at Columbia would expect—a prestigious position with Bankhaus Steiner, which hid her true affiliation with the CIA, a great apartment in Vienna, a great guy in her life who she was head over heels for. Not that Cole knew she was in love with him. He was the type who would probably get scared away if she declared those three little words. An ache swelled in her heart, a yearning for something just out of reach.

Impatient with herself and Cole's current silence, she snatched up her phone. If Cole hadn't called or texted, that likely meant he didn't have anything new to share, but someone had to know what was going on.

She pulled up her contacts and debated her options. Choosing the most direct route first, she dialed Marit's number. No answer. Assuming Cole would call when he could, that left only one other person who would likely have news before her. Lars.

She pulled up his number and pressed the Call button.

He answered on the fourth ring with a breathless hello.

"Lars, I'm so sorry to bother you, but I was hoping you'd heard something from Marit."

"I talked to her a few hours ago." He paused, and the distinct click of a door closing carried over the line, followed by the chime of a bicycle bell. "Why do you ask? Is she not answering your call?"

"I haven't talked to her at all since the police picked her up."

"The police?" Alarm sounded in his voice. "What police?"

Isabelle gripped the phone tighter. "I'm sorry. I assumed you knew."

"You assumed I knew what?" Lars pressed. "Is Marit okay?"

"As far as I know. She left a message for Cole that the police had taken her in for questioning."

Lars paused again. "I don't see any missed calls or messages from her." Another stretch of silence. "Why would she call Cole and not me?"

"I don't know. Maybe she figured Cole would be able to get some answers about why they were taking her in."

"Sorry, Isabelle, but I've got to go." A sense of urgency carried in his voice. "I need to call Marit."

"I just tried. She isn't answering."

"And you don't have any idea why the police took her in?"

"No. Cole is looking into it." Isabelle glanced at the large clock on the wall. Eight o'clock. "In fact, he should have answers for us anytime now."

"I'll call Cole, then."

"I'm sure they'll both call as soon as they can."

"I'm heading home from work right now. As soon as I've packed a bag, I'll head for the train station. There's got to be a train leaving for Paris tonight."

"Lars, I'm sure Cole will handle whatever problem Marit is dealing with. You should get some sleep. Take the train in the morning."

"I'm not going to be able to sleep until I know Marit's okay."

Isabelle could relate to that. "I bet we'll hear something soon," she assured him. "But do me a favor. Call me if you hear anything."

"I will. Same goes for you," Lars insisted. "Call me the minute you hear from Cole."

"I will. I promise." Isabelle ended the call and lowered the phone in her hand to her side. Poor Lars. That hadn't gone the way she'd planned.

The moment Lars hung up with Isabelle, he called Marit. He waited, his chest tightening as the ringing continued unanswered until it connected to her voice mail.

"Hey, Marit. It's Lars." Mentally scrambling for the right words, he opted for simplicity. "Call me. I'm worried about you."

Disconnecting the call, he gazed down the darkened street. He'd exited Coster Diamonds through the rear door. Headlights—bright on the passing cars and twinkling like stars on the bicycles—swathed the shadows, illuminating the empty spot where the armored vehicle had been parked only fifteen minutes before.

He took a steadying breath. The jewelry was inventoried, loaded, and on its way to Paris. There was nothing at work that was pressing enough to prevent him from leaving too. And if Isabelle was right and Marit was in trouble, that was exactly what he was going to do.

His bicycle was chained to the bike rack a couple of meters away. Fifteen minutes to ride back to his flat, half an hour to change his clothes and pack his bags, twenty minutes for a taxi to take him to Centraal Station. If there was a train running this late at night, he could be on his way to Paris within an hour.

Filled with new urgency, Lars pulled up the train schedule on his phone. He scanned through the departures, and his heart sank. The last train for Paris today had left at nineteen fifteen, and the next one wasn't until eight fifteen tomorrow. That was far too long to wait for news.

He pulled up Cole's contact information and pressed Call. Not surprisingly, the call rolled directly into Cole's voice mail. His cousin was either on the phone or had it on Do Not Disturb. Knowing Cole, it was the latter. Not bothering to leave another message, Lars ended the call and slid his phone into his pocket.

Battling a fresh wave of frustration and concern, he crossed the short distance to his bike, unlocked the chain around the front wheel, and grimly pulled his bike free. He'd use the extra time tonight to double check that he had all the photography equipment he needed, take out the rubbish, and email Coster's secretary to inform her of his change of plans. Going to bed didn't even make the list. If Marit didn't return his call to tell him she was okay—and why she'd called Cole instead of him—he'd be doing a whole lot more pacing than sleeping tonight.

Cole rushed into the second police station, irritated on principle with his experience at the last one. Had the officer at the reception desk been forthcoming sooner, Cole would have known he was at the wrong location and that the local authorities weren't willing to help him find Marit. He should have called in a favor and pinged her phone when he'd first found out that the police had taken her in.

With a quick glance at the waiting area, Cole took in the dismal scene before him. The room's hard plastic chairs were either dingy gray, or they were white and desperately needed a cleaning. He wasn't sure which, nor did he care. He wasn't going to sit around waiting this time.

He approached the reception desk, prepared to do battle if that was what it took to get some answers. Of course, he'd need to find someone fluent in English to wage a war of words.

"*Excusez-moi. Parlez-vous anglais?*" he asked in his best French accent.

"*Oui.*" He said something else, but it took Cole a minute to decipher the words through the thick accent. "May I help you?"

"I'm here to see Marit Jansen," Cole said. "She was brought in for questioning around four thirty this afternoon."

Before the man could respond, movement sounded behind him, and Marit's voice carried to him. "Cole?"

Cole whirled around, relieved that Marit was visibly unharmed. "What happened?"

Marit's only response was to close the distance between them. She wrapped her arms around him, and her body trembled.

Cole returned the hug. "It's okay." He looked around the waiting area to ensure she didn't have a police escort waiting to snatch her away. A smattering of people occupied the dingy chairs, but none of them were in uniform, and none were armed. But the man sitting in the corner, holding a camera, could be dangerous for different reasons. Probably some beat reporter looking for a story for tomorrow's paper. Cole doubted that he or Marit would be of interest since neither of them had committed a crime. And at the moment, the man's camera was in his lap, not pointed in their direction.

"Are you good to leave?" Cole asked.

"I'm just waiting for them to bring me my purse and phone." She eased out of his embrace.

It was a good reminder. Cole should call Isabelle and give her an update, but that would have to wait until he had more answers and he and Marit didn't have an audience. "How long have you been waiting?"

"I don't know. Fifteen minutes. Maybe more."

"Let's see if we can speed them up a bit." Cole turned to the reception officer again and mentally prepared to deal with their language barrier as a result of his own limited French. Marit stepped beside him, and he opted for a better solution. "Tell him we want to know how much longer it will be before your belongings are returned to you."

Marit nodded and spoke to the man in French.

"*Je ne sais pas.*"

Cole didn't need a translation for the I-don't-know response. "Ask him to check for us. Tell him I'm your attorney, and I'm here to take you home."

Marit translated again.

The officer gave Cole an appraising look before he lifted the phone and dialed. Then, as though Cole had caused him the greatest inconvenience of all time, he spoke in rapid French to whoever was on the other end of his call. He paused, spoke again into the phone, and ended with "*Merci.*" He gave Cole a pointed look before speaking to Marit. "*Vos possessions seront retournées dans un instant.*"

"*Merci.*" Marit took Cole's arm and tugged him away from the counter.

"What did he say?" Cole asked.

"He said my belongings will be returned in a moment."

Sure enough, less than two minutes passed before an officer approached the desk. "Marit Jansen?"

"Yes." Marit lifted her hand and approached the counter, where the new arrival now stood.

He said something else in French and passed a clipboard and pen to her.

Marit signed her name and traded the clipboard for her purse and cell phone.

Cole motioned her toward the door. "Come on. Let's get out of here, and you can fill me in on what happened."

Cole approached the taxi he had left waiting for him and pulled open the back door. He waited until Marit slid in and he'd taken his place beside her before he asked, "Have you eaten?"

"No."

"Then, let's take care of that before we go back to your flat."

"Dinner would be wonderful, but I should probably call Lars first and let him know what's going on."

Cole gave the driver an address and put his hand on hers before she could dial. "I know you want to talk to Lars, but I need details if I'm going to help you, and the quickest way to lose your perspective is to talk to someone who will feed into your emotions."

"He'll be worried that he hasn't heard from me yet."

"Text him, then. Let him know you'll call him later." That would give Cole the chance to get the details firsthand without stressing Lars out about his girlfriend not calling back.

Marit debated for a moment before she let out a sigh and heeded his advice.

Cole followed her lead and sent a quick text of his own to Isabelle. *I'm with Marit. I'll call later.*

Marit looked up from her phone. "Where are we going?"

"A little restaurant around the corner from where you're staying. I didn't want to have to grab another cab tonight, and I'd rather not take you on the Metro after what you've been through."

"That sounds perfect."

"Now, tell me everything."

Marit drew in a deep breath and let it out slowly. "I'm not sure exactly where to start."

"How about telling me why the police took you in."

"Apparently, there was a theft." Marit glanced at their driver and lowered her voice to a whisper, leaning close. "It was at one of the designers' offices where I went yesterday for a fitting."

"Did they think you were a witness? Or were you a suspect?"

"I'm not sure."

"How long did you have to wait before they questioned you?"

"I don't know. They took my phone, so I didn't have a way to keep track of the time, but it was quite a while, at least several hours."

"You were a suspect, then."

"Me?" She lifted her hand to her chest.

Cole looked up at their driver before straightening. "You can tell me the rest of the story when we get to the restaurant."

Ten minutes later, their driver pulled up at their destination. Cole paid the man in cash—no need to leave an electronic trail of his presence here—and opened the car door. He did a quick check of the street before he motioned for Marit to join him on the sidewalk.

Placing his arm protectively around Marit's shoulders, he escorted her inside, where more than half the tables were still occupied, despite the late hour. He spoke to the hostess, made his standard apology for not speaking French, and requested a corner table along with an English menu.

Once they were settled at their table and they'd given their orders, Marit finished her account.

"It sounds like the man you saw in Ralph's office is the person the police should be looking for."

"I think so too," Marit said. "It was either him or the custodian." She paused. "Or the other people who were on the floor who I didn't see. I heard voices, but I couldn't tell where they were coming from."

"Let's start with the man you saw." Cole pondered how quickly he could get this situation resolved so Marit would no longer be of interest to the police. "What's your schedule like tomorrow?"

"I have fittings starting at eight and a casting call in the afternoon."

"We should call Ralph first thing in the morning to get his employee's name," Cole said. "I'll track him down while you're working."

"That's a good idea."

"In the meantime, I'd rather you not be alone tonight. Do you have a couch I can sleep on?"

"I won't be alone. I have a roommate."

"Good. That will make it less awkward for me to stay at your place."

"That won't work," Marit said. "Even if I wanted to, we aren't allowed to have guests. Our building is for models only."

"Then, I'll pretend to be a model."

Marit stifled a laugh. "Sorry, Cole. You might have the tall, blond, and handsome thing down, but you don't walk or talk like a model."

"How hard can it be?"

"First, you'd need to learn how to walk into a room without looking like you're going to shoot someone."

"I know how to do that. I go undercover all the time."

She shook her head. "Even if you could pull it off, the male models aren't allowed on the upper floors."

"Why?"

"It's the whole *appearances* thing. No designer wants any of their models caught in a negative light of any kind, especially during Fashion Week."

"Your safety needs to be our priority."

"I'm sure I'll be fine," Marit said. "After all, the police let me go, and my building has a security guard in the lobby twenty-four hours a day."

"I'd still feel better if I were close by."

"There are a few hotels on the same street as the building where I'm staying. Maybe you can get a room at one of those. There may still be some rooms available since Fashion Week hasn't started yet."

"Fine. I'll get a room at one of the nearby hotels, but I'm getting a room there for you too."

"Why? I have a place to stay, and like I said, I have a roommate."

Cole lowered his voice and leaned forward. "Yes, but your roommate isn't armed. I am."

Marit didn't speak for a moment. Finally, she nodded. "Okay. You win."

Their server arrived with their food. After he set their dinner on the table and left them alone, Cole pulled out his phone. "Want to help me look for a hotel while we eat?"

"Considering you traveled to Paris because of my phone call, it's the least I can do."

CHAPTER 5

A HOT MEAL AND COLE'S comforting presence had done wonders to restore Marit's equilibrium. Her interaction with the police was over—hopefully for good—and she was ready to put the whole interrogation incident behind her.

Cole held open the restaurant door, the light from within spilling onto the pavement outside. "Are you okay walking from here to the hotel?" he asked.

"Yes," Marit answered. "Like you said, it's not far. But do you mind if I call Lars as we walk?"

"Go ahead." Cole guided her around a couple strolling slowly arm in arm.

Marit pulled out her phone. Three missed calls. Two from Lars and one from Isabelle. She glanced at Cole. "Does Isabelle know you're in Paris?"

"Yeah. I called her from the train."

"You might want to give her an update. It looks like she tried to get ahold of me."

He nodded. "I'll call her as soon as you're safely in your room."

"You don't have to wait on my account," Marit said.

"It's okay. I'd rather wait until I have the privacy of my hotel room."

Marit pulled up Lars's number.

He answered on the first ring. "Thank goodness! I've been really worried about you. Are you okay?"

"Yes," she said, touched by the obvious concern in his voice. "I'm fine."

"Isabelle called and told me you were taken in by the police for questioning. What happened?"

Marit glanced behind her. Other than Cole, no one was close enough to overhear her. "I don't know much. It has something to do with a theft at one of the fashion houses I visited yesterday. They made me wait in a room by myself for a long time and then asked me a lot of questions before letting me go."

"I'm so sorry, Marit. I hate that you had to go through that on your own. You should have called me." He paused. "I heard you called Cole instead."

"They only allowed me one call, and Cole was the first person I thought of who might know what to do if things didn't go well at the police station."

"Yeah." She caught the wryness in his tone. "Most of us don't frequent those kinds of places as often as he does."

Fighting back a smile, she glanced at Cole. He raised a questioning eyebrow, but she didn't take the bait.

"We're headed to a hotel right now," she said. "Cole's insisting that we stay in neighboring rooms tonight."

"Tell him thanks for me," Lars said, genuine relief in his voice.

"I will." She paused. "Can I call you tomorrow, after we've both had some sleep?"

"How about I see you tomorrow instead?" Lars asked.

She gasped. "I thought you were arriving on Friday."

"Yeah, well, when your girlfriend gets pulled in for questioning by the police, you change your plans," he said. "If there'd been a late-night train, I'd be there right now, but I'll be on the first one out of Amsterdam in the morning."

This time, Marit did nothing to hide her smile. "Really?"

He chuckled. "Really. I should be there by nine thirty."

"I have a break between fittings at ten. Can we meet for brunch around ten thirty?"

"Absolutely."

"How about Bistro 24?" Marit asked. "It's just off the Champs-Élysées."

"Sounds great."

A flurry of excitement rose above her exhaustion. "I love you, Lars. I can't wait to see you."

"I love you too," he said. "Stay safe. I'll be there soon."

He disconnected the call, and Marit lowered the phone from her ear. "Lars is arriving tomorrow morning," she told Cole. "We're meeting for brunch at ten thirty at Bistro 24. Do you want to join us?"

"Yeah," Cole said. They'd reached the hotel's entrance, and he pulled open the door. "What time do you leave for your first appointment?"

"I'm meeting Esmee in the lobby of the flat building at half past seven. I should probably be there half an hour earlier to clean up and change. We have to be at Camille Allard's fitting by eight."

He nodded. "I'll walk over there with you. Text me when you're ready to go in the morning."

"As much as I appreciate your help tonight, you don't need to escort me tomorrow too," Marit said.

"Until we know exactly what the police are investigating and Lars is here to take over, I do," he said firmly.

Marit was too tired to argue. "Thanks, Cole."

"Happy to help." He guided her toward the check-in desk. "Come on. Let's get our keys and see if they can find you a toothbrush."

Isabelle opened her laptop on her dining room table and checked her calendar for the next few days. Nothing on it demanded that she be in the office, and if the silence stretching out between her and Cole was any indication, Marit's issue with the police was more serious than they'd first thought.

Isabelle paced to the hall closet and pulled out her go bag. Might as well make sure she could leave quickly if the need arose.

Then again, maybe Cole would call and tell her everything was fine and that he was coming home.

That thought had barely formed when her phone rang and Cole's name lit up her screen.

"What happened? Is Marit okay?" she asked the second she answered the call.

"She's fine," Cole said. An elevator chimed in the background.

Relieved that everyone was safe, Isabelle asked, "Where are you?"

"I just checked into my hotel."

Padded footsteps carried over the line, followed by the beep of an electronic keypad opening. Isabelle waited until the click of a door closing sounded before she pressed Cole for details. "Why did the police take her in?"

"She was a suspect in a robbery. We aren't sure what was taken, but the theft happened around the time she left the offices of a designer who is here for Fashion Week."

"Have the police cleared Marit?"

"They didn't have enough evidence to hold her, but I don't think she's off their list yet," Cole said. "From what she told me, I think she may have seen the culprit."

"That's scary."

"Yeah. I'm not thrilled that I can't crash on her couch to make sure no one comes looking for her."

Isabelle shook her head as a smile started to form. Cole had no clue how that might look to anyone outside their close circle of friends. "I doubt her agent would be thrilled with that arrangement."

"Apparently, her building won't let it happen anyway. All the flats there are for models." Cole sighed. "Marit doesn't think I could pass for one."

Isabelle's smile broke free, but she managed to cover her quick burst of laughter with a cough. "If her building is that strict, I'm sure they have security in place."

"A concierge with a security vest at the front door isn't my idea of tight security," Cole said. "That's why I convinced her to stay at my hotel tonight, until I can check out her flat for myself."

"Not many places would live up to your standards," Isabelle said dryly.

"I'm sorry I didn't make it home tonight," Cole said, changing the subject. "I really did try."

"It's okay," Isabelle said, though she couldn't deny her disappointment. "Any idea how long you're going to be in Paris?"

"No. I told Marit I'll meet her in the morning to escort her back to her flat and then to her fitting. I'm also hoping to meet up with the designer to see if I can shake any new details loose."

"You realize you don't have any jurisdiction in Paris, right?"

"Not technically, but I have an ID with me that will give me access," Cole said. "I want to stay in Paris until the police have the real thief in custody, and the sooner that's taken care of, the better."

"If Marit already pointed a finger at a new suspect, that could happen by tomorrow." Isabelle walked back to her laptop and glanced at the calendar displayed on the screen. "You know, I could grab a flight tomorrow, and we could spend a few days in Paris."

"What? Like a vacation?" Cole asked.

"Yeah. We could try to catch Marit at one of her shows, maybe see the sights." Isabelle sat at the table and looked at her calendar again. She could definitely pull a long weekend away from work. With the amount of leave she had saved up, she might even be able to manage to stay for all of Fashion Week. "What do you think?"

Silence hummed over the line for several seconds. Isabelle drew her eyebrows together. Did he have another mission pending that he hadn't told her about?

"Cole?"

"There's a direct flight that leaves at eight tomorrow morning. Will that work?"

Both relieved and delighted, Isabelle nodded to the empty room. "That sounds perfect."

"Great. Marit and Lars are meeting at ten thirty for a late breakfast/early lunch. I'll text you the address. We can all meet there," Cole said. "Or better yet, I'll text you the address of my hotel. You can leave your luggage in my room until we get you your own."

"Sounds good. I'll meet you there."

"I can't wait."

CHAPTER 6

No one was in the narrow hall when Marit exited the lift on the fourth floor of the models' flats the next morning. With a promise to be fast, she'd left Cole waiting outside the building's front door. If she could manage it, she wanted to be back there before Esmee showed up.

Hurriedly unlocking the door to her temporary home, she turned on the light. Her breath caught. Half the kitchen cupboards were open. The sofa cushions were askew, and the pile of brochures they'd gathered for sight-seeing ideas were scattered across the coffee table and had spilled onto the floor.

The feeling of vulnerability Marit had experienced while waiting in the police interrogation room flooded back. Forced to acknowledge that her recent experience had rattled her more than she'd thought, she attempted to tamp down her instinctive panic. Perhaps she was overreacting. She had nothing to do with whatever the police were investigating, which meant there was no reason whatsoever for someone to break into her flat.

She glanced at Nadia's bedroom door. It was closed. Was she still asleep? Did she know anything about this mess?

Marit crossed to her own bedroom. Here, too, all the drawers were open, and in the closet, her suitcase lay with the lid up, the shoes she'd left inside now scattered. She stared at the bedding heaped on the floor, a deepening sense of unease trickling down her spine.

A door clicked. Marit swung around. Nadia entered the flat, her eyes narrowing the moment she spotted Marit.

"Want to tell me what happened last night?" Nadia said, folding her arms.

Was Nadia referring to Marit's time at the police station or the state of the flat?

"What do you mean?" Marit asked.

"The flat." Anger flashed in Nadia's eyes, and she unfolded her arms long enough to wave one in the general direction of the living room. "You trashed it."

Marit stared at her. "You can't seriously think that I did this!"

"Well, I didn't. And there isn't anyone else here."

Marit moved away from the bedroom door. "Does your room look like my room?"

Giving her a puzzled look, Nadia stepped close enough to peer into the room Marit was using. "Yes," she said warily. "But I have clothes strewn all over the floor too."

What felt like a large-sized rock settled in Marit's stomach. "I didn't do it, Nadia. I give you my word."

Nadia must have believed her because in an instant, her expression went from challenging to fearful. Her brown eyes darted to the flat's front door. "I slept on the sofa next door last night because I was so mad at you. But you think someone else came in here? Someone who went through all our stuff?"

"It looks that way," Marit said. "I was here for a few minutes around four o'clock, but then I left again. What time did you get in?"

"About eight," Nadia said. "I was with a group of girls from the Garnier Agency until then."

"And the flat looked like this when you arrived?"

"Worse," Nadia said. "I cleaned some of it up."

The rock had yet to leave Marit's stomach. She had no idea what this was about, but having her flat ransacked at the same time she was being questioned by the police seemed way too coincidental for comfort. "Are you missing anything?" she asked.

A look of panic crossed Nadia's face, and she disappeared into her room, only to reappear a few seconds later holding a gold watch. She held it up so Marit could see. "It was my grandmother's," she said. "As long as I still have this, I'm okay."

"It's beautiful," Marit said. "But if they didn't take that, they probably weren't looking for valuables." She gazed out at the untidy heap of brochures on the living room floor. "And if that's the case, what were they looking for?"

"I don't know," Nadia said. "But we have to tell Esmee."

"Yeah. And I have a friend who needs to know too."

"Who?"

Marit glanced at the clock on the wall. "His name's Cole, and he's meeting us downstairs in twenty minutes. Grab your stuff. The sooner he and Esmee know about this, the better."

Cole stood outside Marit's building, his gloved hands in his pockets, his pistol concealed in the holster at the small of his back. He hoped he wouldn't have to use it while here in Paris, but his decision to take the train so he could keep his weapons gave him a sense of security that he was grateful for right now.

Marit walked outside with another model, who had dark, curly hair. Marit started toward him but stopped when a well-dressed older woman joined them. Marit greeted the woman, who appeared to be in her early fifties, before continuing forward.

Cole met Marit halfway. "Are you ready?"

Marit nodded. "Cole, this is Nadia, and this is our agent, Esmee."

"Good to meet you both." Cole shook hands with each of them before speaking to Marit once more. "Where are we off to?"

"I'm sorry, but outsiders aren't allowed at the fittings," Esmee said.

"It might be best if we let Cole come along," Marit said.

Nadia nodded in agreement.

Esmee looked from Nadia to Marit. "What's going on?"

"Maybe we should talk about this on our way." Marit lifted her arm in the air and flicked her wrist. A moment later, a cab pulled to the curb.

Cole opened the door and waited for the women to slide in.

Esmee looked up at him from the center seat. "We won't all fit."

"We can squeeze," Marit insisted. She climbed in and scooted over to make room for Cole.

Cole sat beside her, barely able to close the door.

Esmee offered a disgruntled shake of her head before giving the driver their destination. "Why must he come with us?" she then asked.

"Because Nadia and I think someone broke into our room yesterday evening," Marit said.

"What?" Esmee and Cole asked in unison.

"Our stuff was everywhere," Nadia said. "Whoever came in went through everything."

"Was anything taken?" Cole asked.

Nadia shook her head. "Not that we could tell."

"Have you reported the break-in to the police?" he asked.

"No," Marit said. "We only realized there was a problem a few minutes ago."

"We need to do that now." Cole motioned toward the building entrance. "The building supervisor needs to know about it too."

Esmee looked at her watch. "We don't have time. If Nadia and Marit miss this fitting, they'll lose the opportunity to walk in one of the biggest shows of Fashion Week."

Cole sighed. *Models.* "Tell me everything you know, and I'll call the police after I drop you off."

With a surprisingly calm voice, Marit said, "It happened after the police arrived at four and before Nadia got back at eight."

"The police?" Esmee shifted her body so she could see Marit more clearly. "What were the police doing at your flat?"

"They had some questions about a recent crime," Marit said. "They thought I might have seen something."

"What crime?" Esmee grasped Marit's hand. "What happened?"

"I'm not really supposed to talk about what the police told me, but Cole came to help me get everything sorted out."

"You should have called me right away," Esmee said, clearly affronted.

"I wasn't sure the police would give me more than one phone call," Marit said, obviously trying to smooth her agent's ruffled feathers. "And Cole was the only person I knew who could sort everything out."

Esmee turned to Cole. "Do you work in law enforcement?"

"I'm with the American Embassy," Cole said. There was no need to specify exactly where the embassy was located. "Marit may not be an American citizen, but she's a close friend, and I have some experience working with the local police."

Esmee's features instantly transformed from irritation to gratitude. "It was very good of you to help."

"No problem," Cole said. "In the meantime, I do think we should consider finding Marit and Nadia somewhere else to stay."

"You don't think the intruder will come back, do you?" Nadia asked, panic in her voice.

"It's better to be safe than sorry."

"Fashion Week starts next week." Esmee shook her head. "All the hotels in this part of the city will already be booked out for it."

Cole bit back his frustration. "This is their safety we're talking about."

"I'll talk to the building supervisor. I'm sure we can arrange to have an extra guard posted."

"Tell him you need the lock changed as well," Cole insisted.

Esmee nodded. "I'll take care of it."

Though not thrilled that Marit would be staying where an intruder had been so recently, Cole forced himself to accept Esmee's solution. No need to mention that he would be looking for other ways to enhance safety measures when he got back to her flat later today.

They arrived at the design house, and Esmee paid the driver while everyone piled out onto the sidewalk. As soon as they entered, Cole ran into another obstacle, this time in the form of a six-foot-two, broad-shouldered security guard. "Sorry. No one goes in unless you're on the list."

Marit shot Cole a look of apology. "I'm sure we'll be safe here."

"She's right," Esmee said. "And I'll stay close to both of them."

Cole debated his options. He could use his Interpol ID to circumvent security, he could sit around in the lobby for the next hour and a half, or he could search for answers. He leaned close to Marit and whispered in her ear. "Where is Ralph Molenaar's office?"

"It's only a block from here," she said.

"Can you text me the address?"

She nodded. "We should get upstairs."

"Text me when you've finished here. I'm supposed to meet Isabelle at my hotel room so she can drop off her bag, but I can come pick you up first if you want."

"Isabelle is coming?" Marit asked, surprise and delight lighting her eyes.

"She lands at nine fifteen."

Esmee stepped forward and put her hand on Marit's arm. "I'll make sure Marit gets to where she needs to go."

"Thanks. I appreciate that." Cole took a step toward the door. "I'll see you at the restaurant."

Marit nodded. "Thanks, Cole."

Cole waited until the three women passed through security and disappeared into a nearby elevator before he exited. He then pulled out his phone and called the police station where Marit had been questioned last night. Thankfully, the officer who answered spoke English and agreed to take the report of the incident over the phone.

After giving him the timeline Marit had provided and passing along his contact information as well as Marit's phone number, Cole headed for the door. With any luck, the police would be able to meet with the building supervisor before Marit returned to her flat this afternoon.

A text chimed on his phone. The address for Ralph Molenaar's offices.

Cole plugged it into the GPS on his phone. Less than five minutes later, he stepped out of the chilly morning air and into the warmth of an expansive lobby. He approached the sleek reception desk. Suspecting the designer wouldn't see him without an appointment, he reached into his pocket and retrieved the Interpol ID the CIA had been kind enough to fabricate for him for situations just like this one. Okay, so maybe the CIA didn't want him to use his fake ID for personal reasons, but Marit was practically family, and it was possible Interpol would end up involved if the theft crossed international borders.

"I need to see Ralph Molenaar."

"Is he expecting you?"

"No, but it's quite important." Cole slid his badge across the counter as though it were just any other ID. No need to draw attention to himself or his reason for coming.

The security guard nodded. "His office is on the sixth floor. I'll let him know you're on your way up."

"Thank you."

Cole crossed to the elevator. When he stepped out on the correct floor, a man stood waiting.

"I'm Ralph Molenaar." Hope shone in the man's eyes. "Do you have news?"

"Not yet," Cole said. "Is there somewhere we can meet privately?"

"My office is this way." Ralph led him down the hall and into his office.

Cole surveyed the room, right down to the cipher lock on the closet door. "Is this where the theft took place?"

"Yes." Ralph motioned for Cole to sit before circling behind his desk. "I don't know how anyone could have gotten the combination."

An electronic code breaker, a magnetic lock pick, or the old-fashioned look-over-someone's-shoulder method. Any of those could have worked.

"Marit Jansen was questioned by the police last night," Cole began. "She mentioned seeing a man in your office when she came back to retrieve a lost glove. Brown hair in need of a trim, young, early twenties."

"That sounds like Brinton James." Ralph's expression clouded. "He didn't report for work this morning."

"Then, it's possible he's your thief."

"I never thought Marit could have been guilty," Ralph said. "She's a sweet girl."

"I agree." Cole waved in the direction of the safe. "What exactly was taken?"

Now Ralph's eyes narrowed. "You don't know?"

"The police report was incomplete when it crossed my desk last night."

Suspicion crept into Ralph's expression. "Are you really working with the police?"

"The local authorities are never happy when outside law enforcement gets involved." Cole drew out a business card that aligned with his cover with

Interpol. "Here's my card. If you search the internet, you'll see that the phone number there is one that belongs to the local Interpol office."

Ralph pulled out his phone, first conducting an online search and then making a call to confirm Cole's identity. Once he was satisfied, Ralph said, "Sorry. You can't be too careful these days."

"I agree," Cole said before repeating his question. "What was stolen last night?"

Ralph drew a deep breath, as though trying to gather his courage. "It was the designs for this year's entire line."

"What format were these designs in?" Cole asked.

"Muslin patterns, and the computer designs on a jump drive." Ralph's expression darkened. "Whoever it was also wiped out my hard drive. I have no way to prove the designs were mine."

"Any idea who would benefit from this theft?"

"It has to be another designer." Ralph raked his fingers through his hair. "My show is on the second-to-last day of Fashion Week. Any designer who goes before me could feature my designs, and I wouldn't be able to do anything about it. I'd be ruined."

Cole didn't understand much about fashion, but corporate espionage was devastating regardless of the industry. "Wouldn't your models be able to say that they've already been wearing your designs if someone else tried to showcase them?"

"They could try." Ralph shook his head. "But with nothing left to prove I created them, to the world, I would appear to be the thief."

"I'm going to do everything I can to find those designs and get them back to you," Cole said. "In the meantime, I need you to take me through everything that happened last night, and I'll need your authorization to release any security feed from the time in question."

A faint glimmer of hope sparked in Ralph's expression. "I'll help you in any way I can."

"Good. That's what I was hoping you would say."

CHAPTER 7

Gare du Nord was busy. Pushing the case full of his photographic equipment in one hand and hauling his duffle bag in the other, Lars wove his way across the crowded railway platform. It would be nice to think that once he made it out of the station, he'd clear the congestion, but he had a sinking feeling that most of these people were headed to the taxi line too.

He walked outside. The skies were overcast, and there was a nip in the air. Pulling his knit hat out of his pocket, he put it on. As expected, the queue for taxis was long. He was going to be here a while.

He thought about texting Marit to tell her he'd arrived, but she probably wouldn't have her phone until her fitting was over, and he'd be seeing her soon after that. Instead, he used his time in the queue to pull up the local news on his phone. Marit had said she'd been questioned about a theft at one of the fashion houses. Would the networks have picked up the story yet?

A protest outside a car manufacturer's plant. Teachers threatening to go on strike. A new baby giraffe at the Paris Zoological Park. He kept scrolling. There had to be some mention of Fashion Week this close to opening day. A couple of photos popped up. The caption under the first one read, "Lila Peters arrives in Paris for Fashion Week." Lars glanced at the candid picture. The Academy-Award-winning actress was walking through Charles de Gaulle airport flanked by bodyguards.

The second caption read: "Popular model Marit Jansen takes time off work to visit the Champs-Élysées with her boyfriend, Lars Hendriks." This photo had been taken at night with the iconic Arc de Triomphe barely visible over the shoulder of the man whose hand was lying protectively on the woman's back. Lars raised a quizzical eyebrow. Even if he and Cole looked enough alike to pass for each other in the dark, that was no excuse for shoddy reporting. Though his cousin wouldn't have appreciated having his name show up in the newspapers, not when he worked so hard to stay off everyone's radar to protect his ability to function in his work with the CIA.

A red banner flashed up on Lars's phone screen, covering the paparazzi photos with the words *Breaking News*. Lars continued to read the headline. *Member of Dutch fashion designer Ralph Molenaar's team found dead in Paris.* Lars's breath caught. Marit said she'd been taken in for questioning over a theft at one of the fashion houses. He knew she regularly worked for Ralph. Had the theft happened at his office? Could the crimes be related?

The young woman standing at the curb, directing the taxi traffic, shouted at him. Lars looked up. The six people in line ahead of him had all climbed into the same vehicle. He was up next. Moving forward, he waited for the ensuing car to stop, and then he opened the door and shoved his case onto the seat. Running around to the other side, he signaled the taxi driver to remain behind the wheel. Lars didn't have time to wait for him to open the boot. He needed to find Marit.

The restaurant had a small front. About a dozen chairs were positioned around four small round tables on the pavement outside. So far, only one hardy Parisian had claimed a seat there. Guessing that Marit would prefer the warmth of an indoor table, Lars pushed open the door and hauled his baggage inside.

A server dressed in a white shirt and black trousers met him. Politely ignoring Lars's cumbersome luggage, she smiled a welcome. "*Bonjour, monsieur.*"

"*Bonjour,*" Lars responded in French. "I'm meeting my girlfriend here, but I'm not sure if she's arrived yet."

"Ah, yes. Is it Marit?"

Relief mingled with excitement. She was here. "Yes."

The server nodded. "Follow me, please."

Navigating his camera case and duffle bag through the tight spaces between the restaurant's chairs, Lars followed the young woman to the back of the room. Marit was sitting alone at a table set for four. As soon as she spotted him, she rose to her feet. Lars dropped his duffle bag on the nearest chair at their table, ignoring the server and the menu she set on the table, and pulled Marit into his arms.

She held him tight, raising her lips to meet his as he pulled her close. "I've missed you so much," she murmured.

"The last twelve hours have been torture," he whispered, reluctantly releasing his hold on her. "And if we weren't standing in the middle of a restaurant right now, that kiss would have lasted significantly longer."

She smiled impishly. "Next time, we'll make sure there's no one else around."

"Deal." He slid his case behind the chair and then waited for her to reclaim her seat before sitting beside her. "You're really okay?"

"Yes." The light in her eyes dimmed slightly. "But I have more to tell you."

He reached for her hand. "What is it?"

The doorbell rang, announcing the arrival of more guests. Lars ignored it, but Marit looked up.

"I'll tell you as soon as Cole and Isabelle join us," she said.

"Cole *and* Isabelle?" Lars turned to see his cousin and his cousin's girlfriend following the server toward their table. "When did Isabelle get here?"

"She flew in this morning," Marit said.

Shaking his head in disbelief, Lars rose to greet Cole as Marit moved around the table to give Isabelle a hug.

"How close to Paris were you when Marit called?" Lars asked Cole.

Cole grinned. "Closer than Amsterdam."

Lars offered him a grateful nod. "Thanks for coming."

"Anytime. I didn't do much more than make sure she ate and walk her to the hotel."

"I saw the photos of you walking her back." Lifting his phone so Cole could see the screen, Lars pulled up the screenshot he'd taken.

Cole frowned. "Where was this posted?"

"On *Le Monde*'s website."

His cousin muttered something under his breath, and then he pulled out Isabelle's chair. "Let's all sit down," he said. "We've got some things we need to talk about."

Isabelle passed her menu to the waitress, a sense of déjà vu washing over her. Although she and Marit spoke often on the phone, she and Cole hadn't seen Marit and Lars since spending a few days together at Falcon Point in early January. And though Isabelle had a few colleagues at the bank who she was close to, Marit was the only real friend she had here in Europe.

"I really wish we didn't live so far apart," she said.

"Me too," Marit said. "And I wish we had a better reason to get together than me getting questioned by the police."

And her room getting ransacked. Cole had filled Isabelle in when she'd met him at his hotel. This quick weekend getaway was feeling much more like a protection detail than a vacation, right down to the motion sensors and security cameras tucked into the bottom of her suitcase.

As though sharing her thoughts, Lars said, "Hey, at least we haven't had to deal with any guns being pointed at us." He shuddered. "I still have nightmares from the last time you were in Amsterdam."

"I still have nightmares from when Beckett found out we borrowed his skis," Cole muttered.

Isabelle stifled a laugh. She didn't know all the particulars of how Cole had ended up using Beckett's brand-new skis at Falcon Point or how they had ended up in Lars's room afterward, but Beckett had chewed Lars out for a good twenty minutes before Anna had come to his rescue.

Lars shook his head. "How did you make him think it was me?"

Cole shrugged. "Sorry, cuz. Some secrets I can't share."

"This isn't exactly espionage we're talking about."

Isabelle glanced at Cole. No, they might not be working as spies right now, but Cole clearly wasn't taking any chances. Otherwise, he wouldn't have a gun holstered at his back and another at his ankle.

"What can you tell us about last night?" Isabelle asked, changing the subject.

Marit relayed her story, beginning with when the police had shown up and ending with when they had questioned her.

Lars put his hand on her back, love and concern shining in his eyes.

Envy shot through Isabelle, quick and fierce, and she fought against it. She loved Cole. She loved her relationship with him, but sometimes she wished to move beyond where they were now, to move into a relationship that included the absolute adoration that was nearly tangible between Lars and Marit.

Marit continued her account, breaking Isabelle out of her thoughts. "They never told me what was stolen, but someone must have seen me around the time the theft occurred."

"It was the custodian," Cole said.

Marit's eyebrows lifted. "Did you talk to Ralph this morning?"

"Yeah. It was definitely an inside job."

"How do you know that?" Marit asked.

"First of all, it's a double-safe system. With the right tools, a pro could probably break through it within an hour or two, but the security cameras didn't show anyone entering Ralph's office after you left, except the custodian, and he was only in the room for seventeen seconds."

"Probably just long enough to empty the trash," Isabelle said.

"Did Ralph tell you what was taken?" Marit asked.

"Yes." Cole looked around the room before he leaned forward and spoke quietly. "He said he lost the designs for his entire line for this year."

"That can't be right," Marit said. "I'm sure he had multiple copies of the computer designs, not to mention the muslin forms."

"It's all gone." Cole shook his head. "The thief stole the designs Ralph put on a flash drive and wiped them off his hard drive. I don't know what those muslin things are, but those are gone too."

"You can't be serious." Marit clearly looked distressed. "The muslin patterns are the master designs. Without those, he can't re-create the clothes he's designed. Especially if he's lost the digital format too."

Isabelle couldn't imagine that an outsider would be able to access Ralph's office and computer, and it seemed even less likely that they would know where everything was located. "It really does sound like an inside job."

Lars took a sip of his water. "Could someone have overridden the security cameras?" he asked. "You know, plugged in a fake feed?" When Cole shot him a look of disbelief, he added, "Hey, I've seen the movies."

"Yeah, they could have. But I checked the security access rooms. No sign of tampering, and there were guard sightings multiple times outside Ralph's office, at least once every half hour. Not many people could get in and out without leaving a trace." Cole leaned in again and lowered his voice to a whisper. "Not to mention, Brinton James, the man Marit saw in Molenaar's office, didn't report to work today."

"Of course he didn't show up for work." Lars focused on Cole. "He was killed last night."

"Wait." Marit grasped Lars's hand. "What?"

Cole straightened. "Where did you hear that?"

"The news broke on it a little while ago. I saw it right after I spotted the photo of you and Marit." Lars pulled out his cell and tapped on the screen. He then passed it to Cole.

Isabelle leaned forward so she, too, could read the article. "They didn't give many details."

"There probably aren't a lot of details to share yet." Cole's jaw tightened.

Isabelle didn't have to hear Cole's thoughts to share them. Someone involved in Monday's theft was eliminating witnesses, and Marit could be next.

"Marit, maybe you should consider staying with me while we're here in Paris," Isabelle said.

"Where are you staying, Isabelle?" Lars asked.

"I'm not sure yet, but it might be best to keep you out of sight, especially after what happened last night."

Concern lit Lars's eyes, and he focused on Cole. "You think she's in danger?"

"I don't know what to think," Cole said. "But I'd like to know who was in her flat last night and what they were looking for."

Lars whirled to face Marit. "Someone was in your flat? Why didn't you say anything?"

"We didn't realize it until this morning." Marit squeezed Lars's hand. "Nadia thought I left a mess, and Cole insisted I get a room at his hotel last night, so I had no idea until I went to grab my stuff before my fitting."

"Then, Isabelle's right. You need to stay somewhere else," Lars said. "Either that, or Cole and I are crashing in your living room."

"I appreciate the offer, but as I already told Cole, men aren't allowed on the upper floors, and the entire building is for models only."

"Then, we'll find a place we can all stay together," Cole said. "I have a friend who might have a flat we can borrow."

"I appreciate that, but even if I can convince Esmee, I'm probably more vulnerable when I'm going to fittings and casting calls than when I'm in my flat."

"She's right." Isabelle hadn't been around the modeling scene for years, not since one of her best friends had entered the circuit for a brief two years of crazy travel and had ended up finishing high school online. On the two occasions that Isabelle had accompanied her to New York's Fashion Week, the backstage area had been complete chaos.

"We need someone with Marit who can access everywhere she goes," Isabelle continued.

"I'll have backstage access at the Ralph Molenaar show because of the Coster jewels his models will be wearing," Lars said. "Other than that, I have media access, and that's it."

Cole shifted his attention to Isabelle for a moment; then he exchanged a long look with Lars, one that communicated something without words being spoken.

"What?" Isabelle asked. "Do you have someone in mind?"

"Oh yeah." Cole nodded. "What do you think, Lars?"

"I've always said Isabelle could pass for a model."

"Me?" Isabelle shook her head. "I've never modeled. And I haven't been backstage at a fashion show since I was a teenager."

"You're infinitely more qualified than either of us." Cole wiggled his thumb, indicating himself and Lars.

"I don't want Isabelle to be in danger because of me," Marit said.

"I'm not thrilled about the idea myself," Cole said, as though he didn't know she had the same basic CIA training that he did. "But we all know she has great self-defense skills, and she can handle a gun."

Marit lowered her voice to a whisper. "I doubt Isabelle brought a gun."

"No, but I have a spare," Cole said.

Despite Cole's declaration, doubt colored Marit's expression. "Look, I know it seems like all I do is walk up and down a runway, but it's way more involved than that."

"She's right." Isabelle nodded vehemently. Just the thought of stepping out in front of hundreds of people made her stomach turn. "Women work for years to get a shot at modeling in Paris, especially during Fashion Week."

"You can do this," Cole insisted. His gaze fixed on hers, and Isabelle didn't miss the plea reflected there. "Especially if Marit is willing to help you."

"We don't have enough time for Marit to help me," Isabelle insisted. There had to be another option.

"That's true," Marit said. "Casting has already started."

"It's worth a try." Lars took Marit's hand. "Isabelle is a natural athlete. We've seen her fight. With your help, I bet she can do it. And we don't have any better options."

Marit seemed to consider the possibilities. "Esmee won't go for me staying somewhere else. We already tried that." She sighed. "It seems crazy, but maybe Cole and Lars are right."

"Maybe they're not," Isabelle said. "I don't know the first thing about how to prep for a casting call."

"But I do," Marit said. "And I think I know how to make it possible for you to stay at the flat with me too."

"How?" Isabelle asked.

Marit pulled out her phone. "Give me two minutes, and keep your fingers crossed."

The waitress returned with their food.

As soon as she left them, Marit dialed. "Esmee? Remember when I did you that favor last Christmas and worked during my holiday?" She paused briefly. "Now it's my turn to ask a favor." Marit focused on Isabelle. "I need you to put a friend of mine on the list for the rest of the casting calls I'm going to." She paused, and the indistinct buzz of a woman's voice carried over the phone. Marit tensed. "You've seen her photo already. She's the one who was with me at Schönbrunn Palace in Vienna last fall. She was wearing the blue silk Monique Marin with the lace overlay."

Now a little smile flitted over her lips. "Yes, that's her. Auburn hair. Gorgeous green eyes."

Isabelle's jaw dropped as the full force of Cole and Lars's plan hit her. They were all nuts! She wasn't a model.

Another pause, and more buzzing coming through the line. Sincerity filled Marit's voice when she spoke again. "I wouldn't ask if it weren't important."

A flash of victory crossed Marit's features. "Thank you so much. Her name is Isabelle Rogers." Another pause. "Perfect." Marit's mouth curved into a grin. "Oh, and one more thing. Isabelle is going to be rooming with me."

Marit paused again, the woman's voice coming in a steady hum now.

Finally, Marit nodded. "Thanks, Esmee." She hung up. "We'd better eat. Isabelle and I have a casting call at noon."

"Oh, no." Isabelle shook her head. "Pointing a gun at someone is one thing. Stepping onto a runway is way beyond me."

Marit reached across the table and put her hand on Isabelle's. "I meant what I said earlier. It won't take me long to teach you the basics, and with how fast you pick things up, that's probably all you need."

Battling a new kind of apprehension, Isabelle looked down at the chocolate croissant on her plate. Somehow, she didn't think she was off to a very good start.

CHAPTER 8

Marit led Isabelle into the ransacked bedroom. Despite the reassuring words she'd offered Isabelle at the restaurant, unease over what lay ahead gnawed at her frayed nerves. She pointed at the twin bed next to the one she'd been using. "Go ahead and leave your bag there. I haven't had time to clean up yet, but we'll make some space in the closet after we've been to casting."

Isabelle lowered her bag onto the bed and surveyed the room. "This is what you came back to last night?"

"Yeah." Marit suppressed a shudder.

Isabelle walked to the window. She examined the casement and peered outside.

"It's pretty unlikely that an intruder would come in through the window," Marit said. "He'd have to be Spider-Man to have scaled that wall to the fourth floor." She grimaced, remembering that someone had actually entered Isabelle's fourth-floor window in Vienna that way once. "I think he somehow made it past the concierge downstairs and had access to the lift and our door key."

"It looks that way," Isabelle said. "The fire-escape stairs wouldn't grant easy access. They're on the other side of the building."

It wasn't the most comforting observation, but right now, Marit had other, more pressing concerns than ready access to the fire escape. She glanced at the time on her phone. "We have twenty minutes before we're supposed to meet Esmee downstairs. If we're going to get you backstage with any of the designers, we need to focus on what the casting agents will be looking for."

"You know?" A sliver of hope shone in Isabelle's worried eyes.

"In general, yes. And Lars wasn't kidding, Isabelle, you have the look. You just need to add the right moves." She walked into the living room. "Come here. I'll show you." Marit positioned herself at the front door and waited until

Isabelle was standing in the center of the living room. "One of the first things the agents are going to ask you to do is to walk for them."

"Why does that sound terrifying?"

Marit laughed. "Just forget they're watching and focus on the way you move your body." She straightened into a familiar pose. "Back straight, core tight, shoulders back and down."

"Back straight, core tight, shoulders back and down," Isabelle repeated, imitating Marit's position.

"Great. Now your arms." Marit began walking. "They should swing slightly, and your hands should be relaxed. Your arm movement helps keep your pace steady."

"And I have twenty minutes to get this down?"

"Sixteen," Marit said. "But you can totally do this. Try it from there."

Taking a deep breath, Isabelle assumed her starting pose and started to walk.

"Good," Marit said. "Remember to keep your shoulders relaxed, and try not to move your hips too much. They should remain straight."

Isabelle made it as far as the bedroom before making a half turn, just as Marit had done. She groaned. "Why isn't Cole or Lars doing this?"

"Because they aren't women. Besides, they wouldn't make it through the wait in line, let alone receive a call back," Marit said, moving to stand beside her. "You've got this. You already look better than most of the new models out there. This time, let's do it side by side."

They walked across the room together two times before Marit had Isabelle walk it alone again. She adjusted the tilt of Isabelle's chin once and the length of her stride twice. By Isabelle's fifth time across the short distance, Marit knew her friend's aptitude for picking up new physical skills was not limited to self-defense.

"That was fabulous!" Marit said, clapping her hands. "Seriously, Isabelle. I'm really impressed. Add one of your beautiful smiles and you'll be on every callback list you try for."

"It's going to be really hard to smile while I'm trying to remember everything I'm supposed to do with my arms, chin, hips, feet . . ." Isabelle looked at her with an uncharacteristic hint of panic. "Women train for years to work the Paris Fashion Show. Not twenty minutes."

"True," Marit said. "But some women are naturals, and some will never get it no matter how hard they try. You, my friend, are a natural. I'm not exaggerating how well you're doing. You may not feel comfortable with it yet, but no one would ever guess you've never modeled before."

"It's a lot harder than it looks. And even though you're a great teacher, with so little practice . . ."

Marit shook her head. Now was not the time for Isabelle to lose her confidence. It would manifest itself in the way she moved. "You've got this, Isabelle. You really do."

Isabelle still didn't look fully convinced, but she mustered a smile. "I'll do my best."

It was a big ask; Marit knew that. She gave Isabelle a hug. "Thanks for being willing to try."

"Let's just hope your agent approves of me."

"She will." Marit grabbed her bag. "It's time to go, so let's head downstairs, and I'll introduce you."

Esmee and Nadia were already in the lobby when Marit and Isabelle arrived. They saw Marit exit the lift and walked over to meet them.

"Esmee and Nadia," Marit said, "this is my good friend Isabelle Rogers. Isabelle, my agent, Esmee Scheffer, and my colleague, Nadia Muller."

"Nice to meet you," Isabelle said, extending her hand to Nadia and then to Esmee.

Nadia gave her a polite smile, but Esmee eyed Isabelle critically. "You were right, Marit." She released Isabelle's hand and circled her slowly. "Flawless skin, green eyes, thick hair, long legs, and a good figure. She certainly has potential."

If Esmee had not been completely serious in her physical assessment of Isabelle, Marit would have broken down in a fit of giggles at the look on Isabelle's face. As it was, Marit bit her lip to contain her laughter and offered up a silent prayer that Isabelle would not be so affronted by the blunt appraisal that she would walk away.

"I . . . I think so too," Marit managed, and then, tucking her arm through Isabelle's, she tugged her toward the door before her friend had a chance to voice a response. "I see Cole and Lars waiting for us outside, and if we don't want to be late, we'd better head over to Henri LaRue's casting session right now."

Cole really needed to find time to spend with Isabelle that didn't involve police, guns, and undercover work. As it was, he and Lars stood outside the design house and waited for Isabelle and Marit to disappear inside.

Isabelle cast a panicked look over her shoulder.

Cole mouthed the words, "You'll be great."

Marit must have picked up on Isabelle's nerves, because she wrapped her arm around Isabelle's shoulders and guided her forward.

"They're going to be okay, right?" Lars asked from where he stood beside Cole on the sidewalk.

"Yeah." *They'd better be.* Cole wasn't crazy about Isabelle taking an active role in protection duty, but she was armed with his spare weapon. Plus, she was never without her wicked right hook. Cole hoped she wouldn't need either method of defense anytime soon.

He supposed he should be grateful that Lars and Marit had accepted the idea of Isabelle sticking close to Marit for protection. Even though neither of them was aware of her employment with the CIA, they had both witnessed her skill with a pistol and her self-defense abilities.

"What now?" Lars asked.

"We find a new hotel room." Cole had completed his checkout and was now saddled with hauling his go bag around with him, never an optimal situation. The hotel from last night had been two blocks from Marit's flat—two blocks too far away.

Cole headed for the nearest Metro stop. "Where are you staying while you're here?"

"I haven't made a reservation for tonight yet." Lars pulled out his phone and tapped on the screen before turning it toward Cole. "Here's the info for the place where I'm supposed to stay. Hopefully, they'll let me check in a couple of days early."

Cole checked the address and nodded his approval. "This is perfect. It's right next to Marit's place."

"That makes sense. She's the one who recommended it."

"We'll try there first."

Ten minutes and one transfer later, they arrived at the hotel. Cole studied the exterior while Lars headed for the door.

Marit's building was directly next door. If he were lucky, Cole could get a fixed vantage point to help him choose a room facing Marit's building. He continued past the hotel to the corner. When he looked down the crossroad, the Eiffel Tower came into view.

Lars caught up to him. "What are you doing? The hotel's that way."

"I just needed a little perspective. Come on." Cole entered the lobby, where a man around Cole's age stood behind the counter. "We need to check in."

"Name?"

"Hendriks," Lars said. "My reservation doesn't start for a couple more days, but I arrived early."

The clerk frowned slightly. "We're very busy at the moment, but let me see what we can do for you." The man tapped on his computer keyboard. "Ah, yes." He nodded. "It looks like you requested a superior double room, and there is actually one available. Shall I add the extra days to your existing reservation?"

"Yes," Lars said. "That would be great."

"Any chance we can get a room facing away from the Eiffel Tower, preferably on an upper floor?" Cole glanced at Lars. "With two beds?"

Though surprise crossed the desk clerk's face, he simply tapped a few more keys. "I will need a credit card and your IDs please."

Lars and Cole handed over their passports, and Lars gave the clerk his credit card.

After the clerk went through the typical ritual of checking them in, he handed them their passports back along with their key cards. "You're on the sixth floor. The lift is behind you to the left."

Cole pocketed his passport and grabbed the keys. "Thank you."

They found the elevator, one of those old-fashioned ones barely big enough for the two of them with their luggage.

Cole led the way inside and hit the button for the sixth floor. "Let me know how much the room is, and I'll split it with you."

"My work is paying for the days that I had to be here anyway. We can just split the extra days," Lars said. "What's the plan once we drop off our bags?"

"I need to shake some intel loose," Cole said. "I want to know what the police have on the victim and the crime scene."

The doors slid open on the sixth floor, and they made their way to their room.

Lars unlocked the door and stepped inside. Two twin beds were pushed into the center of the room, only a foot of space between them. A table for two was nestled beneath the tall window on the far side of the room, with barely enough room to pull out the chairs.

"This is cozy." Lars slid his duffel and his equipment case to the side of the bed nearest the bathroom.

"It'll do." Cole closed the door behind him and pulled out his cell phone. He dialed his boss's number.

Jasmine answered on the third ring, her Southern accent carrying in her words. "I was wondering when I was going to hear from you. Is everything okay with Marit?"

The fact that Jasmine knew Marit's name was a reminder that his personal and professional lives had crossed far too often when Lars and Marit were around. "I'm not sure. The man she ID'd at the site of the theft turned up dead today. Think you can shake loose the police report for me?"

"Name?"

"Brinton James," Cole said. "While you're at it, maybe you can get the report from the theft too. I'd like to know if this guy was involved or if he was a witness."

"Let's hope it's the first scenario."

The one where Marit wasn't next on a kill list. "Oh, I am."

"I'll put the request in, but you know how the locals can get when we try to interfere," Jasmine said. "Marit isn't a US citizen, so we don't have any real reason to be involved."

"I know. That's why I'm hoping you can also run the guy's last known address for me."

"That's easy enough. I'll pull it up and text it to you."

"Thanks, Jazz."

"You can thank me by staying out of trouble."

"I can do that."

"I'll pretend like I believe you." Jasmine laughed. "Any idea how long you'll need to stay in Paris?"

"Worst case, through the end of Fashion Week," Cole said. "Marit has Isabelle going on some casting calls with her. Looks like she may get roped into working some shows."

"Isabelle modeling?" Jasmine asked with a little too much enthusiasm. "Oh, you have to take pictures."

"I'll pass that job off to Lars. It's his thing."

"Good idea," Jasmine agreed easily. "I'll forward those police reports as soon as I get them."

"Thanks again." Cole ended the call. He dropped his go bag on his bed. He'd barely set it down when his phone rang. Jasmine. "Don't tell me you couldn't find the guy's address."

"Oh, I found it, but I doubt you're going to find many clues about his murder at his apartment in Amsterdam."

"I guess it makes sense that he's just here for Fashion Week since he was working for a Dutch designer."

"I'll text you the address of the hotel where he was staying. You can use your FBI credentials to gain access. I'll clear your name through the local FBI legal attaché."

"What good will that do?" Cole asked. "Like you said, Marit isn't a US citizen."

"No, but Brinton James is."

"You're kidding."

"No. Based on his residency permit application, he moved to Amsterdam nine months ago to apprentice under Ralph Molenaar. Before that, he was a student at The Fashion Institute of Technology in New York."

"Thanks, Jazz. That intel will open a lot of doors."

"Use those open doors wisely," Jasmine cautioned.

"I will." Cole ended the call.

"What did she say?" Lars asked. "I mean, the part you can tell me about without having to kill me afterward."

"James is a US citizen who was living in Amsterdam."

"I didn't expect him to be an American."

"Me neither." Cole headed for the door. "I'm going to check out where this particular American was staying here in Paris. Maybe there will be a clue about why he was killed."

"Want me to come with you?" Lars asked.

"You'd better stay here." Cole didn't need his cousin present while he broke into a potential crime scene.

"What am I supposed to do while you're gone?"

"How about putting that fancy camera equipment of yours to work?" Cole pointed to the window. "Pretty sure we should have a perfect view of the entrance to Marit's building."

Lars crossed the room and stared through the glass. He turned, awareness evident on his face. "This is the reason you didn't want a view of the Eiffel Tower."

"Yep."

"I'll set up my tripod."

"Call me if you see anything unusual."

"I will." Lars set his camera case on his bed and unzipped it. "And, Cole?"

"Yeah?"

"Thanks again for coming."

Cole nodded. "No problem." He hoped.

CHAPTER 9

Isabelle couldn't believe she was doing this. Dozens of models waited in the large room, each of them taking turns walking down a center path, then taking a turn to the right, and heading back to the left before exiting through a door a short distance behind her.

The croissant she'd eaten an hour ago had turned into an uncomfortable mass in her stomach. She doubted the yogurt Marit had eaten had settled much better.

Marit put her hand on Isabelle's back and nudged her forward. "You're going to do great."

Isabelle lowered her voice. "I feel like I'm going to throw up."

"The first look is always the hardest. Consider this a practice run."

Isabelle drew a deep breath in an effort to settle her nerves and the nausea churning inside her. It didn't work. She needed a distraction, like figuring out who was behind the theft so she wouldn't have to step on a runway in front of an audience.

"Is the show for this designer before or after the one for Ralph?"

"Before."

"What about the other shows you're already scheduled for?"

"Dior and Chanel are on the last day," Marit said. "I only have two others already booked. One is on opening day. The other is the next day."

"Which ones are those?" Isabelle asked.

"Camille Allard and Peter Wade." Marit kept her voice low. "They're both still casting. Esmee should be able to get you auditions. I told her to only put you up for auditions that happen before Ralph's show."

"When did you talk to her about that?"

"When you were getting your bag from Cole's hotel room," Marit said. "We have this one and two more later this afternoon."

"I don't know if I'll survive *one* of these, much less three."

"Just pretend we're back in the flat," Marit said. "Shoulders back, chin up, and pretend everyone in the room is Cole right after he woke up."

"You want me to pretend all these people are my boyfriend with unruly hair?"

Marit nodded. "The whole picturing people in their underwear is just too weird."

Isabelle laughed. She couldn't help it.

"You're next. Are you ready?"

"No."

"You can do it," Marit encouraged. "It's all about attitude. Go out there like you belong, and you will."

A woman stood at the front and took Isabelle's name before snapping a photo. She then motioned her forward.

Isabelle moved to what, in essence, was the top of the runway. Attitude. It was all about attitude.

She lifted her chin, straightened her back, and started forward, lengthening her stride the way Marit had taught her. A pivot turn halfway down the runway, followed by a second so she would once again be facing the right direction. A T-stop when she reached the end, before turning to the right. One more turn and a handful of steps to the left. Then it was over.

Isabelle swallowed the sigh of relief that fought to escape. It wouldn't do for the others in the room to witness how grateful she was to have that over with.

A man in his early twenties held up his hand to stop her from going beyond him. He looked over her shoulder, then nodded at someone behind her.

"Name?"

"Isabelle Rogers."

The man handed Isabelle a small slip of paper. "Your callback is tomorrow at ten."

Isabelle's jaw dropped, but she recovered quickly. "Thank you."

She continued toward the exit, turning around in time to watch Marit walk the runway, a little smirk on her face, her hips swaying just enough to showcase the silk pantsuit she currently wore. Confidence and poise. Marit had both in spades.

Isabelle waited by the door for Marit. When Marit joined her, she, too, carried a little white piece of paper.

Marit's gaze lowered to Isabelle's hand. "You got a callback?" Marit asked.

Still in shock, Isabelle nodded.

Marit hugged her. "I knew you could do it!"

Together they walked out into the hall, where Nadia already waited with Esmee. Nadia also held a callback slip.

"Well?" Esmee asked.

Marit held up the evidence of her success. "So far, so good."

Esmee's gaze landed on Isabelle's hand. "Excellent." She nodded toward the exit. "Come on. We have another appointment in thirty minutes. I don't want my three stars to be late."

"You mean two stars," Isabelle said. "I'm just along for the ride."

"You're one of Esmee's girls now." Esmee lifted her chin a little higher. "That means you're one of the best."

"I only got a callback," Isabelle said.

Esmee cocked an eyebrow. "On your first audition at Paris Fashion Week."

Marit draped her arm around Isabelle's shoulders. "We'll wait until after the next two casting calls before we tell you what a big deal that is."

Isabelle swallowed hard. "Good idea."

Cole reached the address Jasmine had texted him. A van with police markings was parked in front, likely a forensics unit. He'd rather hoped the local detective would still be on site, but that possibility had been a long shot at best. If the murder had hit the papers and the forensics team was processing the scene, the lead detective would have already gone through the procedures of logging his report and notifying the next of kin.

Cole bypassed the front desk and headed for the elevator as though he were a guest rather than a visitor. When he reached the correct floor, he stepped into the hall and located James's room.

Even if Jasmine hadn't given Cole the room number, it would have been hard to miss the yellow crime-scene tape crisscrossed over the door.

Cole knocked and pulled his FBI credentials from his pocket. An officer opened the door, a fingerprint brush in his hand.

Cole held up his badge. "Cole Bridger, FBI. *Parlez-vous anglais*?"

"*Oui.* I am Lieutenant Tremblay." The man in his forties narrowed his eyes. "What do you want?"

"I'd like to take a look at the crime scene. The victim was an American."

The man leaned closer to inspect Cole's badge. "Very well. We have almost finished."

Cole stepped over the lower piece of crime-scene tape and ducked his head to avoid the piece strung across the top of the door. "How long will it take to process the fingerprints?"

"A few days. Maybe more." Lieutenant Tremblay walked through the narrow entryway, past the bathroom to his left.

Before Cole reached the main part of the room, he caught sight of a dresser pushed against the wall. All the drawers hung open, and clothing lay strewn across the room. Cole continued forward to where another man stood with a camera in hand.

Lieutenant Tremblay said something in French. Cole caught the mention of the FBI and guessed that he was explaining Cole's presence to his partner.

"Did the room look like this when you got here?"

"*Oui.*" Lieutenant Tremblay pointed at the suitcase lying on its side beside the luggage rack. "Someone was looking for something."

"Do you think they found it?"

Lieutenant Tremblay shook his head. "Doubtful. Whoever it was tore through every bit of clothing and every drawer."

Which meant the lieutenant was probably right. If the culprit had found what he was looking for, the search would have stopped when he'd found his prize, leaving part of the room untouched.

"Is this where James was killed?" Cole asked.

Lieutenant Tremblay waved at a spot on the floor beside the window. "Right here."

Cole continued forward until he spotted the blood on the carpet. Judging from the single blood stain that spanned at least a foot in diameter, Cole guessed the victim had been killed by either a knife or a bullet that had hit an artery. "Cause of death?"

"Gunshot wound to the chest." Lieutenant Tremblay shook his head slowly. "No doubt that someone wanted him dead."

"Any witnesses?"

"I'm not sure. You'll have to ask Capitaine Dupont about that."

"Do you have his number?" Cole asked. If Jasmine didn't gain access to the police report by tonight, he might need to hurry it along himself.

Lieutenant Tremblay pulled a business card from his pocket. "You can call the main number there. They can patch you through."

"Thanks." Cole scanned the room again. First Marit's apartment was searched. Now James's hotel room. What was the intruder looking for, and why would he or she think James or Marit had it?

Cole's gaze landed on the suitcase, and he instinctively looked for the messenger bag James had been carrying when leaving Ralph's office last night. When he didn't see it, Cole pulled a pair of crime-scene gloves from the small pocket beside where his gun was holstered. He tugged them on and opened the closet door. Clothes covered the floor, and the safe door was open, but there was no bag.

"Did you see a blue messenger bag, about this big?" Cole held up his hands eighteen inches apart.

"I haven't seen it." The lieutenant translated the question to his partner, who shook his head and spoke in rapid French.

When he finished, Lieutenant Tremblay said, "We've inventoried everything. It's not here."

"Any chance it was already logged into evidence?"

"I don't think so, but if it was, it will be in Capitaine Dupont and Brigadier Blanchet's report."

"Thanks. I'll check with them." Cole pulled an FBI business card from behind his ID badge and handed it to the lieutenant. "Can you please send me your crime-scene photos when you finish?"

"As long as the detective approves, I'll send them."

"Thanks. I appreciate it." Cole took a couple quick photos of the room before shaking Lieutenant Tremblay's hand. "I look forward to hearing from you."

Cole stepped toward the door, surveying the mess still in front of him. He didn't know if James was guilty of theft or had simply been in the wrong place at the wrong time, but whoever was searching rooms was missing something. Whether it was Ralph's designs or something else, Cole didn't know, but one thing was apparent: Brinton James had been killed in cold blood, and it was up to Cole and Isabelle to make sure Marit wasn't next.

CHAPTER 10

Lars zoomed in on the elegant Parisian woman walking her dog past the entrance to Marit's building. He snapped a picture. Whoever said dogs and their owners looked alike was definitely on to something. A long, narrow nose and white curls pulled onto the top of her head—the description of the woman could be used for her giant poodle too.

They continued down the road, and Lars studied the assortment of new photos on his camera. He'd taken several candid shots of passersby, but as far as he could tell, the only people who'd entered Marit's building since Cole had left were half a dozen young women, who looked to be models, and a locksmith. He'd taken close-up shots of the locksmith and his assistant along with their van that boasted the name of the company and a phone number. It shouldn't be too hard to check their legitimacy.

His phone buzzed. He picked it up. A text from Cole.

Leaving the hotel now. Stopping to pick up Isabelle and Marit. Want to grab dinner for all of us? We could eat at our place.

Dinner in Paris. And he got to choose the menu. He grinned. He'd pick up some kind of vegetable to appease the girls, but eating something loaded with spinach was not happening on his watch.

On it, he texted back. Then he pulled up a list of the takeout restaurants closest to their hotel and started scrolling through his choices.

Three-quarters of an hour later, Lars was unloading the last of the cardboard containers onto the table in the hotel room when he heard the lock click.

"Hey," he said, setting down the carrier bag to greet Marit, Isabelle, and Cole as they entered the room. "How did it go?"

"Isabelle was unbelievable," Marit said, smiling as she moved into his embrace. "Three casting sessions, three callbacks. Esmee was thrilled. She thinks she's discovered a new rising star."

"Pretty sure it was beginner's luck," Isabelle said. "And I think I'll stick with studying a screen full of spreadsheets. It's much less stressful than strutting down a catwalk in front of fashion industry professionals."

Lars couldn't think of much that sounded more boring than studying spreadsheets—except maybe watching surveillance videos—but he understood Isabelle's reluctance to be the center of attention at a fashion show. Standing behind the camera was a much more comfortable place to be. "Well, it's great that you made the cut," he said. "What happens next?"

"Callbacks and fittings," Marit said. "Tomorrow will be another busy day."

"You know," Cole said, thoughtfully, "taking a look at the schedule for the next few days and for the Fashion Week shows themselves might not be a bad idea."

"What are you thinking?" Isabelle asked.

"Ralph mentioned that if another designer showcased the stolen designs before he had a chance to launch his line, it would be almost impossible to prove that they were his concepts first. It seems to me that one way to start eliminating designers from the suspects list would be to take off any of the ones scheduled for shows after Ralph Molenaar's. Our crook would want to be up first."

"Good idea," Lars said, drawing Marit toward the table. "But I vote we eat before we go over the schedule."

"Agreed," Isabelle said with feeling. "Whatever calories I consumed at brunch disappeared in nervous energy during the first casting."

"What did you pick up?" Cole asked.

"Crepes," Lars said. "I have a variety of fillings, from chicken, mushroom, and béchamel sauce to ham, egg, and swiss cheese to ratatouille."

"What?" Marit raised her eyebrows in mock disbelief. "No Nutella?"

"Oh, yeah. I have those, too, but I figured we're supposed to eat the other ones first."

Cole chuckled. "Sounds great."

Isabelle and Cole took the two chairs at the table, and Marit and Lars sat on the edge of the nearest bed, holding their food on paper plates. For a few moments, they each focused on their meals.

"Nice work, Lars," Cole said, breaking the silence. "That hit the spot."

"You haven't even had a Nutella one yet," Lars said.

"It still may happen," Cole said, pulling out his phone, "but there's a pâtisserie three doors down from here, so I'd better pace myself."

Isabelle rolled her eyes, and Marit giggled.

Cole ignored them both, his attention on his phone screen. "Hmm. Ralph told me his show is on the second-to-last day. It looks like there are five shows after his."

"Marit already told Esmee to only have me audition for shows before Ralph's," Isabelle said. "How many are before him?"

"There are usually at least twenty-five shows," Marit said. "That leaves fifteen to twenty that will go before Ralph."

Cole ran his fingers through his hair. "That's a lot of suspects."

"We're going to have to come up with another way of sifting through them," Isabelle said.

"Any ideas?" Lars asked.

"Not yet," Cole said, a familiar look of determination glinting in his eyes. "But they'll come."

Paris at night. With a sigh of pleasure, Marit looked out at the reflected lights dancing across the surface of the Seine and the brilliantly lit Eiffel Tower standing sentinel on the other side of the river. Lars's arm tightened around her, and she set her head on his shoulder, soaking in the wonder of this moment. This beautiful evening stroll was what she had envisioned—had hoped for—when she'd first heard that Lars would be joining her here.

"It's magical," she said. "And I'm so glad you're here to experience it with me."

He pressed a gentle kiss on the top of her head. "Me too."

They stood quietly for a couple of minutes, taking in the iconic scene even as droves of tourists passed by. Work had brought her here, and she was grateful. She loved her career and the opportunities it provided, but she loved the man standing beside her even more. It wasn't the view that made the evening so special; it was sharing this moment with Lars. Truth be told, she wanted to share every moment with Lars.

"Do you want to take a photo?" Marit asked.

"I probably should, huh?"

She smiled as he released her to lift the camera hanging around his neck to his eye. He would take more than one, but it made her happy that he'd seemed as reluctant as she was to end their enchanted moment together.

"And then we can head over to the bridge and catch up with Cole and Isabelle," he added.

Marit looked left, where the pavement joined the Pont Alexandre III bridge. Lamps shone above the decorative stone balusters that ran the full length of the structure, illuminating the crowds of people gathered there. Voices and laughter filled the air. Men standing above cheaply made trinkets and souvenirs called to passersby, urging them to buy an illuminated plastic Eiffel Tower or a glow stick.

"Do you know where they are?" Marit asked. The two couples had arrived together, but it was proving hard to keep track of each other among so many people.

"Yeah." Lars lowered his camera and took Marit's hand. "They stopped a couple of meters onto the bridge. I saw Isabelle pointing out something to Cole through my camera lens."

"Great." Repositioning the straps of her oversized purse on her shoulder, Marit stepped away from the low retaining wall. "It shouldn't take us long to meet up again."

Weaving through the milling tourists, they crossed the short distance to the bridge, but by the time they reached the spot where Lars had seen Cole and Isabelle, the couple had moved closer to its center.

"I understand why they stopped here," Lars said. "That's a great view." The beams of light emanating from the top of the Eiffel Tower swung in a slow circle, piercing the dark night sky above and the iridescent water below. He glanced at her. "Can I have you in this photo?"

With a laugh, she released his hand and stepped up to the balustrade. "Only for you."

Lars grinned and raised his camera.

He'd taken three or four shots when a man rushed by, knocking Lars's elbow and jostling the camera as he passed.

"Hey!" Lars exclaimed.

Ignoring him, the stranger in dark clothes and a dark knit hat lunged for Marit's bag, yanking it off her shoulder. Pain shot down her arm as he tugged it free, and almost before Marit knew what had happened, he was running away with her purse under his arm.

"Cole!" Lars yelled, whipping his camera strap off from around his head and thrusting the camera at Marit before taking up the chase.

Up ahead, Cole and Isabelle swung around. The man darted into a crowd of teenagers, but he wasn't fast enough. Cole had spotted him. Lars had already shortened the distance between him and the purse snatcher, but Cole and Isabelle were closer. They took off in unison, racing around the teenagers as Lars sprinted along the path the thief had taken.

Forcing herself to push past her shock, Marit chased after them. The man broke through the other side of the group, and Cole didn't hesitate. Launching himself at the thief, Cole barreled into the purse snatcher's right side. The man stumbled, giving Isabelle time to reach him.

"Not this time, mister!" She grabbed Marit's bag and pulled it out from under his elbow as he was still trying to catch his footing.

Righting himself first, Cole dove for the thief's arm just as Lars appeared beside him. Cole's fingers connected with the thief's sleeve, but it wasn't enough. The man twisted, and Cole lost his grip. An authoritative shout was followed by the pounding of feet on the bridge. The crowds parted, and without a backward glance, the thief bolted.

Lars started after him, and a new fear struck Marit. To take on a purse snatcher among tourists was one thing. To follow him into the dark alleys of Paris was something else entirely. "Stop, Lars," she called.

He spun around. His face registered his surprise, and he crossed the short distance between them in six long strides. "Marit! I thought you were still where I left you."

"Don't go after him." She wrapped her arms around him. "He knows these streets much better than we do, and he might not be working alone. Isabelle has my purse, and that's the most important thing."

"As much as I hate to admit it," Cole said as he and Isabelle joined them, "she's right." He gave the thief's escape route one last frustrated look before settling his attention on the two uniformed men who'd just arrived at the center of the bridge. "It looks like the police were alerted to what was going on. Are you up for answering their questions?"

A nearby couple was talking to the officers. They pointed to Marit, Lars, Isabelle, and Cole. The officers turned toward them, and Marit's heart sank.

Pulling away from Lars, she braced herself for another difficult conversation. "The local police are going to have my contact information on speed dial by the time I leave Paris."

Isabelle gave her a sympathetic look and handed back her purse. "I'm sorry, Marit. But at least this time, you won't have to face them alone."

It was true. And the thought was remarkably reassuring. "Thanks, Isabelle," she managed a weak smile. "Over the next couple of days, maybe we can mix some self-defense lessons in with our modeling lessons. I think it's time I worked on those skills."

Isabelle gave her hand a supportive squeeze. "Absolutely."

CHAPTER 11

Isabelle still couldn't believe Marit had nearly lost her purse after everything she had already been through over the past two days. Walking ahead of Isabelle, Lars had his arm firmly around Marit's shoulder, Marit's free hand clutching her bag tightly to her side.

Isabelle had opted to go without a purse tonight, her wallet, Chap Stick, and cell phone secured in the zipped pocket of her overcoat. Cole also had his hands free, except for the one holding hers.

The walk along the Seine had been so perfect up until the purse snatcher had shown up. They were due for a break.

"What are the chances that Marit would end up with her name on three police reports in two days?" Isabelle asked, her voice low.

"Until I got her call, I would have put the chances at zero for her name being on *one* police report." Cole squeezed her hand. "I'd feel a lot better if you and Marit would move over into our hotel."

Isabelle had entertained similar thoughts, enough to call and inquire about booking a room. "Your hotel is sold out until after Fashion Week."

"You called?"

"Yes, while I was waiting for Marit and Nadia after the second casting call." Isabelle shrugged. "I needed something to distract me from the thought of going through a third one."

"I know this isn't what you had in mind for this trip, but thanks for helping out."

"Marit's a good friend," Isabelle said. "Besides, she would do the same thing for me."

"That's true," Cole said. "Have you talked to your boss about taking some extra time off?"

He was speaking of her boss at the bank, not Jasmine. "I had already warned him that I might take the whole week off, but once Marit and Esmee started taking me on casting calls, I asked to stay here through Fashion Week."

"He was okay with that?"

"Yes. Even after taking time off during the holidays, I still have a good deal of unused leave on the books."

"That's a good thing," Cole said as they approached Marit and Isabelle's building. "Do you know if Esmee got the locks changed?"

"No, I don't, but we'll find out soon enough." She wasn't sure what Cole would do if the locks hadn't been taken care of. She didn't particularly want to find out.

Cole stopped at the corner, his grip on her hand encouraging her to do the same. As soon as Isabelle faced him, he said, "I'm going to head over to the embassy and pick up some motion sensors and security cameras. The batteries in mine are all dead after my last mission. I'll call you as soon as I get back."

Isabelle glanced at Lars and Marit, who now stood by the entrance. Despite the several meters between them, she lowered her voice. "No need. I brought some with me."

Cole lifted his eyebrows. "You brought some with you?" he asked.

"I didn't know what I'd find here, and I thought it best to be prepared."

Cole gave a slight nod. "How many cameras did you bring?"

"Four. I'll set them up in the hall and in the living room to cover the door and the balcony."

Admiration and a look of approval flashed on his face. "Send me the access code, and Lars and I can take turns watching the feed."

"That would be helpful." Isabelle sighed. "I'm exhausted."

"I bet." Cole glanced over her shoulder before he lowered his head and kissed her.

The moment his lips met hers, her insides melted, and she leaned into him. Cole lifted his hands to frame her face. Her arms encircled him, her fingers brushing against the edge of the holster at his waist.

Despite the reminder that neither of them was exactly what they appeared to be to the world around them, she couldn't help losing herself in the moment. They were in Paris together, the Eiffel Tower glowing in the distance. The love she felt for him swelled within her.

A tingle rippled along her skin, goose bumps forming. When he finally pulled back, he lowered his forehead until it pressed gently against hers. "I'm glad you're here."

"Me too."

Cole gave her another kiss. "Try to get some sleep."

"What about you and Lars? You need sleep too."

"Lars and I can take naps when you're doing your modeling thing."

Modeling at Paris Fashion Week. Isabelle might never have aspired to such a feat, but she was well aware that this was a dream for many in the modeling industry. "I don't know whether to hope I can get these jobs or pray that I don't."

"The more jobs you get, the more access you have to Marit."

"And the more likely it is I'll spot any possible threats." Isabelle sighed. "I really do need to go to bed early."

"Do me a favor when you get to your flat and stand next to a window. I want to see if you're on the hotel side."

"We are." She furrowed her brow. "Are you planning to spy on us?"

"I'm hoping to make sure no one can use any outside access to get to your room."

"It sounds better when you say it that way." Isabelle stepped back. "I'll see you in the morning."

"Call if you need anything."

"I will." Isabelle leaned in for one last kiss before she continued to the door that Lars currently held open for Marit.

"Ready?" Marit asked.

"Yeah." Isabelle and Marit made their way up to the fourth floor. When they stepped out of the lift, Esmee was heading toward them. Nadia followed behind her, a large bag over her shoulder and a roller carryon suitcase behind her.

"What's going on?" Marit asked.

Esmee held up two old-fashioned keys. "The locksmith was here earlier. Here are your new keys." She handed them to Marit. "Nadia is taking the spare bed in Monica's room so you and Isabelle have the flat to yourselves."

"Any chance there are other available beds somewhere else in the building?" Isabelle asked. Switching rooms wouldn't hurt.

"Sorry. Nadia took the last spot," Esmee said, "but the building supervisor did add an extra guard for tonight."

At least that was some improvement.

"We'll see you in the lobby at eight in the morning. Don't be late." Esmee moved past them. "And call me if you have any problems."

"Thanks, Esmee." Marit continued past Nadia and unlocked the door.

Isabelle put her hand on her shoulder. "Do you mind if I go in first?"

"You're sounding like Cole," Marit said.

"He may have rubbed off on me a bit." Isabelle stepped inside before she drew the gun from her purse. Keeping the pistol pointed at the floor, she checked out the bathroom, living room/kitchen space, and the two bedrooms.

She secured her weapon and called out, "It's all clear."

Marit hurried inside before closing and bolting the door behind her. "I'm not sure a new lock and an extra guard in the lobby is going to help me forget someone broke in here yesterday."

Isabelle crossed to the window and pulled the curtains aside. She called Cole, who picked up a moment later. "I'm standing in the window."

"I see you. Look up two floors to your left."

Isabelle lifted her gaze to where Cole and Lars stood behind the glass of a sixth-floor window. "Hey, Marit. Come here."

"Is there someone out there?" Marit hurried forward.

"An extra layer of protection." Isabelle pointed at their boyfriends' room.

"They aren't planning to stay up all night to watch our window, are they?" Marit asked.

"They're taking turns." Isabelle moved away from the window and spoke into the phone again. "Make sure you and Lars get some sleep."

"We will, but don't forget to set up your security measures," Cole said.

"I'll do that right now." Isabelle hung up and crossed to the bedroom to retrieve the equipment from her suitcase. She located the hard-sided silver case and carried it back into the living room.

"Did you want your own room now that Nadia isn't staying with us?" Marit asked.

"Actually, it might be better for us to stay in the same room," Isabelle said. "That is, if you don't mind."

"I was kind of hoping you would say that." Marit's shoulders relaxed slightly. "I know it's silly, but I'll feel better knowing that if I hear something, I can look at the bed beside me and know whether it could be you."

"I get that." Isabelle set the case on the table and opened it. Remembering that Marit had worked for her father's security company as a teenager, Isabelle pulled out three of the cameras. "Want to set these up to cover the door and the windows?"

"Sure."

"Thanks. I'll set up one in the hall so the guys can see our front door," Isabelle said. "And then we can decide where we can set up the motion detectors without tripping them every time we need to go to the bathroom or fix something to eat."

Marit held up one of the cameras and focused on Isabelle. "Thank you for being here."

"Of course." Isabelle hugged Marit. "This is what friends are for."

Marit laughed. "I hate to break it to you, but most friends don't know how to disarm gunmen or set up surveillance equipment." She eased back and looked Isabelle in the eyes. "Unless they work for the CIA or something."

Isabelle's pulse quickened. Suddenly, unexpectedly, she was on dangerous ground. Schooling her expression into a somewhat natural smile, she laughed. "You'd think so, wouldn't you?" She paused, needing to deflect the conversation. "You already have the surveillance part down. How about we work on teaching you how to disarm gunmen? If I can do it, you can do it."

Marit gave a resigned nod, and Isabelle's tension eased a fraction.

"I'll learn that gun trick you do if you promise it means I'll never have to use it," Marit said.

"I'll certainly hope for that," Isabelle replied. And she meant it. Just as much as she hoped that Marit wouldn't revisit her suspicions about Isabelle's involvement with the CIA.

CHAPTER 12

Cole set his laptop on the little table by the window, angling his chair so he could see both the screen and Isabelle's window. He clicked on the link Isabelle had emailed him to access the digital feed from the cameras she'd set up.

Cole turned as Lars lowered into a chair behind him, his camera in hand. "I don't think you'll be able to get many good shots with your camera now that it's dark."

"I got some great ones of the Eiffel Tower." Lars held out his camera so Cole could see the view screen.

Cole stared at the photo, the Eiffel Tower illuminated, the branch from a tree framing it on one side. "That's incredible. You could print and sell that."

"Thanks." Lars scrolled through before he turned the view screen toward him again. "I think this is my favorite though."

In it, the Eiffel Tower rose above the bridge, but somehow, Lars had captured the exact moment Cole had kissed Isabelle in the center of it. Warmth swelled inside Cole, the depth of his feelings expanding uncomfortably. For the first time, he had someone in his life who was more important than anyone or anything else. A burst of clarity pulsed through him as his future unfolded before him, Isabelle at the center of it.

He didn't know how it had happened, but sometime over the past few months, he had fallen in love with her.

Lars shot him a quizzical look. "Are you okay?"

"Yeah." Maybe. He motioned to the photo. "Can you send me a copy of that one?"

"No problem. I'll email it to you as soon as I download these." Lars retrieved his laptop and returned to his seat. "Too bad I chased after the guy who took Marit's purse without taking his photo."

"Seeing as he was wearing a hat, the back of his head probably wouldn't have told us much." Cole narrowed his eyes. Why had the thief gone for Marit's bag instead of Lars's camera? He shook that thought away. He was probably looking for quick cash, not an expensive item he would have to pawn.

Grateful for a distraction from his newfound feelings for Isabelle, he glanced at his computer screen again. Isabelle and Marit had done a nice job of placing the cameras. One covered the window of a bedroom. Another revealed the back half of the living space, including the window they had looked out a short while ago. His other two views were of the door, one from inside the kitchen and the other from the hall.

Cole pulled up the link on his phone so he could access it on that device as well.

A new email from Jasmine popped up on his screen. The police reports. Finally.

While Lars downloaded his photos, Cole scanned the report on the robbery. Everything lined up with what Ralph had told him, right down to the timeline of when the suspected theft had occurred. Two links to security footage were included, each of them spanning a forty-five-minute segment.

"Who's taking first watch on Marit and Isabelle's flat?" Lars asked.

"You pick." Cole motioned to his laptop. "Would you rather watch their building or view security feed?"

As expected, Lars pointed at the window. "I'll keep watch. There's no way I want to get roped into watching security feed."

Cole suppressed a smile. He had hoped Lars would say that. He pulled up the feed of a hallway. The image began with Ralph walking out of his office.

Cole sped it up to eight times speed, slowing it to normal only when someone came into view. James arrived only moments after Ralph left. He didn't emerge again until after Marit arrived eleven minutes later.

Marit left the room, her bag over her shoulder, and James gripped his messenger bag in his hand.

After they disappeared from view, he sped it up again until the custodian entered Ralph's office. As reported, he went in only long enough to empty the trash.

According to the police report, no one else was spotted for the rest of the night.

Cole checked the other security footage, this one of the lobby. He watched this one more slowly, at only four times normal speed so he could identify everyone who came in and out. But no one came in except for Marit, when she went to the elevator to go back upstairs. After she exited, James appeared. He had his bag with him when he walked out, so where was it now?

Cole scanned the rest of the footage. Again, nothing of note occurred after James left.

"I can see why the police questioned Marit," Cole said. "She was the only one who didn't work there who entered Ralph's office. Besides her, only James and the custodian went in during the time frame when the theft occurred."

Lars looked up from his camera, which was once again on the tripod and aimed at Marit's window. "You think James is the thief?"

"It had to be him unless someone overrode the security feed, but the police didn't find any evidence of it," Cole said. "I didn't either."

"If he's the one who stole the designs, then who killed him?"

"I don't know. A partner maybe." Cole pulled up the crime-scene photos from the murder scene. "But if that's the case, those designs might still be out there."

"What do you mean, they might still be out there?" Lars asked.

"Someone tore through James's hotel room, and Marit's room was searched. It makes sense that whoever killed James was looking for something important."

"Something like the designs." Lars leaned back in his chair. "I don't like this."

"Me neither." He eyed his cousin. Lars needed a distraction. "I'm going to run out and grab a piece of cheesecake." Cole stood. "Do you want anything?"

"I thought you were going through security feed."

"I was. I finished."

"Already?"

"I guess I didn't mention that it was only forty-five minutes' worth."

Lars scowled. "No, you didn't."

"I'll bring you back a dessert. We may need fuel if we're going to stay up all night."

"I'm not staying up all night. As soon as you get back, I'm going to bed."

"After dessert."

"Right."

Cole chuckled and grabbed his room key, cell phone, and jacket. When he reached the lobby, he called Isabelle.

"Everything okay?" she asked.

"Yeah." Except for the three little words that were now burning on his tongue. He swallowed them. He couldn't tell Isabelle he was in love with her. No way was he going to risk scaring her off. No, he'd have to wait for her to say "I love you" first. He walked outside and made sure no one was nearby before he continued. "Is there any chance you can pull the bank records for Brinton James? They weren't included in the police report."

"What are you looking for?" Isabelle asked.

"A payoff. I think he may have been hired by someone to steal Ralph's designs."

"I'll take a look."

"I'm heading down the street to grab some dessert. Do you or Marit want anything?"

Isabelle repeated the question to Marit before answering. "Marit said no thanks." Regret carried in her voice when she added, "I'd better skip, too, if I'm going to try this modeling thing this week."

"You're naturally gorgeous. A piece of cheesecake isn't going to change that."

"That's sweet of you to say," Isabelle said. "But if I were to indulge, I'd go for a berry tart."

"Good to know." Cole headed toward the pâtisserie down the street. "Call me if you find anything."

"I will."

Cole pocketed his phone and strode down the sidewalk. He reached the pâtisserie only minutes before closing time and scanned his options, the selections limited because of the late hour. He smiled when he spotted one berry tart left in the display case.

He pointed at the tart and held up one finger. With no cheesecake in sight, he used his limited French and hand signals to order an assortment of pastries, from custard tarts to chocolate éclairs to some fancy pastries he couldn't pronounce. With far more food than he and Lars could likely eat over the next twelve hours, he headed back down the street to his hotel.

He was approaching the door when his phone chimed.

Careful to keep the pastry box level, he pulled his phone from his pocket and read the text from Isabelle. *Meet me outside my building.*

Cole looked up at the same time the door opened, and Isabelle emerged. Cole moved toward her, and she met him halfway.

"You were right to suspect a payoff," Isabelle said. "There was a ten-thousand-euro deposit made into his account two weeks ago."

"Can you trace the source?"

"I'm afraid not." She shook her head. "The deposit was made in cash."

"Ten thousand isn't that much."

"I agree. It was likely intended to be a down payment on the theft," Isabelle said.

A couple approached them, and Cole fell silent until the passersby moved out of earshot. "We have to find out who hired him."

"It has to be someone from one of the other design houses," Isabelle said. "Maybe you should put in a request to headquarters. If you can pull any of the designers' financials, I can look over them to see if anything looks off."

"That's not a bad idea." Cole held up the pastry box and opened it. He pulled out the berry tart. "Here. This is for you."

Isabelle shook her head. "I shouldn't eat this."

"But you're going to."

"You're right." Isabelle took the offered pastry from him.

"Want to pick something for Marit?"

"No thanks. I can split this with her if she wants something."

"Okay, but if you change your mind, let me know. We have plenty."

"You have too much," Isabelle said. "If you and Lars eat all that, you're both going to have stomachaches tomorrow."

"We'll be fine." Cole leaned in and pressed his lips to hers, drawing out the kiss. Forever hovered on the edge of his mind, and he had to fight to keep his thoughts on their conversation. He held up the pastry box. "Trust me. We know how to pace ourselves."

"If you say so." Isabelle gave him another quick kiss. "Thanks for dessert. I'll see you tomorrow."

Cole waited until she disappeared inside before he headed back to the hotel. With any luck, offering Lars pastries would be enough to bribe him to take the first shift so Cole could get some sleep. At least, he would get some sleep after he tried one of those custard tarts. He wasn't trusting Lars to eat just one.

CHAPTER 13

Lars adjusted the height of his tripod as a model approached wearing a navy gown and a necklace that looked very much like the five-carat teardrop diamond pendant he'd help load into the armored vehicle in Amsterdam. The pendant was stunning, but Lars wasn't fooled. Even if he hadn't already known that the models would be rehearsing with costume jewelry, the absence of heavily armed security personnel this morning would have been clue enough. The priceless pieces would stay in the bank's safe-deposit box until right before the actual show.

Lars understood the reasoning behind it, but it didn't make his job any easier. He was basically trying to capture something that still didn't exist. Not only did he have to make a decision on the best way to photograph Coster's jewelry while the models were wearing fake pieces, but he also had to set up his equipment in the rented rehearsal space many of the designers were using rather than at the location of the final shows.

The quality of the lighting would play a huge part in how well his shots turned out. And unfortunately, that would be very different in the Carrousel du Louvre than it was here. Not only would the runway be awash with artificial lights, but they'd also have the natural light coming in from the glass pyramid above them. Of course, that lighting would change according to the time of day and the cloud cover. He shook his head slightly. The whole thing was crazy. He was basically working with a moving target.

The model stopped in front of the small group of photographers and posed. Lars took a few photos, adjusted his zoom, and took a few more.

"Thanks," he said in Dutch.

With an accepting nod, she moved back up the catwalk.

"Who're you with?" the photographer at his right asked, speaking English.

"Coster Diamonds," Lars replied.

"Ah, that explains why you just arrived. You're only here for Molenaar's show."

"Yeah. What about you?"

"I'm with *Elegance Magazine*, based in London." The Englishman gestured to the men at his other side. "*Vogue*, *Elle*, and *Vanity Fair*. We've been here since they started this morning."

Lars did a rapid mental review of the long list of designers he and Cole had scanned through last night. How many of them had been here before Ralph's group? It might be worth a few questions to find out.

"Lars Hendriks," he said, offering the Englishman his hand.

"Tony Watkins. Nice to meet you."

Another model was approaching. Lars turned his attention back to his camera. This one was wearing the ruby earrings with a dress of a similar color. She paused in front of the cameras, and Lars zoomed in on the jewelry. The shutters clicked, and she moved away.

"I'll hand it to your fellow countryman," Tony said. "He puts his models in things that actually look like clothes. Can't say that for all the designers here."

Lars raised his eyebrow curiously. "What else would they be wearing?"

"Good question. Li Du's collection looked like oversized black rubbish bags tied at the neck with holes for the arms and legs."

Lars smothered his laugh with a cough. "Yeah. That sounds a bit weird."

Tony snorted. "They were nothing compared to what Giuseppe Bianchi's models were wearing. I'm just glad the shows are indoors. Fish netting should not be considered a fabric."

Desperately hoping that Marit and Isabelle had stayed clear of that particular casting call, Lars attempted to redirect the conversation.

"How many of the designers have been around today?"

They both paused to take photos of the next model before she moved on.

"At least half a dozen of them," Tony said. "Peter Wade was here. Thinks he's all that, he does. You could hear him yelling at his models from out here. Then there was Camille Allard." Tony shrugged. "Her line was okay but nothing to write home about. Kyle Adams was next. He's supposed to be up-and-coming—at least that's what my editor says. Henri LaRue. He's another one who's a bit off his rocker, if you ask me. Why would he put all these beautiful women in giant hoodies? The only thing that changed from one piece to the other was the color of the fabric and how far down their legs it went."

This time, Lars allowed himself a chuckle. "Not a huge fan of cutting-edge fashion, I see."

"Bonkers, isn't it? I've been doing this gig for twelve years, and I still don't get what all the fuss is about."

Tony bent down to adjust his lens, and Lars looked up to see Isabelle approaching. She was wearing a flowing floral dress and was moving with as much finesse as any of the models before her had.

"This way, please," Tony called to her.

She pivoted in front of the cameras.

"Nice," Tony said.

Lars snapped a shot of the diamond choker at her neck and smiled. No matter what she said to the contrary, Isabelle was crushing this assignment.

"See what I mean," Tony said as Isabelle disappeared. "How many women do you know who want to go out in a black bin bag? That dress was new and fresh and something a normal person would happily wear." He pointed at Marit, who was now walking toward them in denim overalls with red trim. "And that one. See how good she looks?"

Lars's heart warmed as Marit approached. It was no wonder she was a favorite with so many designers. Her natural grace and beauty shone on the runway. And if Lars had his way, it wouldn't be long before she had a diamond ring shining on her left hand as well. He already had ideas for a design that would suit her perfectly. Fortunately, he also had the right connections at Coster to make his sketches a reality.

He heard the cameras click beside him. It was a good reminder of why he was there. Zooming in on the sapphire and diamond studs in Marit's ears, he took a couple of photos before pausing to look up at her. She turned to face him. He winked, and he caught the smile in her eyes right before she made a professional turn and started back the way she'd come.

"I'm telling you," Tony said. "As someone who's been around this business a long time, Molenaar's on to something big. He's making the kind of stylish clothes every woman wants. And the other designers are going to have to scramble if they want to keep up."

Lars reached into his case for a second lens, his thoughts whirling. Was this what was behind the theft at Ralph's office? Had another designer recognized the same thing as Tony, but rather than applaud the fresh direction as the Londoner was doing, had he or she decided to put an end to it by stealing Molenaar's patterns? But what was the ultimate goal? Discredit Ralph as a designer, or beat him to the punch with his own designs?

Tony's insight into the character of many of those in the industry was discouraging, but it was also enlightening. And if Cole could dig up some background information on the designers currently in Paris, they might learn more. Some motivations were easier to spot on a bank statement or after a deep dive into their backgrounds than they were by simply watching someone at work.

He released a tense breath. Marit was more observant than most. If there were any clues to be had in her work environment, she'd likely spot them. And that terrified him. As grateful as he was that Isabelle was backstage with Marit, he hated that the woman he loved was caught in the middle of all this.

Attaching the new lens, he attempted to shrug off his disquiet. With the number of rehearsals and fittings the girls had over the next few days, he and Cole could make use of all that time to look through some not-supposed-to-be-public information on certain designers. Knowing Cole, he'd also be checking police reports. But Lars was okay with that. The sooner they got to the bottom of this, the better.

Isabelle still couldn't believe she was doing this. Seven casting calls in two days, and she had landed five jobs, all of which matched Marit's schedule.

Technically, she had six since being added to Ralph Molenaar's show. How Esmee had managed that, Isabelle wasn't sure, but she was grateful to be behind the scenes for that particular one.

"Isabelle." Peter Wade snapped his fingers.

Feeling far too much like an obedient puppy, Isabelle lifted the long skirt of her current outfit and stepped onto the stool Marit had vacated a moment ago.

Peter stared at the gown, his eyes narrowed. Then he snapped his fingers again. This time, a woman in her early twenties stepped forward.

"Take the hem up a quarter inch." Peter reached out and tugged at the fabric at Isabelle's waist. "And take this in. It should be fitted."

The young assistant hurried forward, pincushion in hand. She quickly adjusted the length before moving to the fabric at Isabelle's waist.

Isabelle stood perfectly still, afraid to breathe for fear of getting stabbed with a straight pin.

Once the adjustments were made, Peter waved his hand. "Next!"

Isabelle stepped off the stool and moved to one of the curtained-off dressing rooms. She changed out of the dress into the slacks and blouse she had put on this morning, then grabbed her purse, opening it long enough to confirm her weapon was secured inside.

Marit approached. "Are you ready?"

"If I say no, can I go back to our flat and take a nap?" Isabelle asked.

"No." Marit shifted her bag more firmly onto her shoulder and hooked her free arm around Isabelle's waist to draw her forward. "Come on. We have the Henri LaRue fitting next."

"More time to pretend to be a human pincushion. Great." Isabelle fell into step with Marit.

"Trust me." Marit weaved past a rack of clothing encased by a black fabric cover. "The designers don't want your blood on their clothes any more than you do."

"It's not the designers I'm worried about." Isabelle brushed past another fabric-covered clothing rack. "It's the pin-wielding assistants who scare me."

Isabelle caught sight of a man in his late forties with thinning black hair. He scowled in their direction, his focus on Marit.

Without pointing, Isabelle asked, "Who's that? The man at my ten o'clock."

To Marit's credit, she barely glanced in the man's direction before returning her focus to Isabelle. "That's Giuseppe Bianchi."

Isabelle recalled the name of the Italian designer coming up when they'd gone over the various designers who had shows before Ralph, but she couldn't remember any details beyond his nationality.

"Any idea why he would be staring at you?" Isabelle asked.

"No clue. I didn't audition for his show."

"Why not?"

"I don't like the way he objectifies women."

Isabelle bristled. "I'm glad that wasn't a show I had to audition for. I'm sure I'd feel the same way."

They reached the spot where one of Henri LaRue's assistants was checking in models. Nadia currently stood on a stool, wearing a bright-pink hoodie that hung well past her hips.

Marit and Isabelle gave their names before moving to their dressing rooms to put on the clothes they had been assigned for this show.

Isabelle picked up the green hoodie that was slightly shorter than Nadia's.

"Believe me," Marit said. "These are much better than Bianchi's short skirts. Plus, we have the added benefit of not needing to accessorize with fishnet stockings."

"I totally owe you for that," Isabelle said.

Marit flashed her megawatt smile. "You're welcome."

Isabelle stepped behind a changing screen and slipped into the hoodie and pair of black jeans that had been laid out for her. After slipping on the white-and-black-checkered Keds that went with the ensemble, she headed toward where Marit now stood on a stool. The way the woman could change clothes so fast was truly remarkable.

"Ah, this is the perfect color for you," Henri announced in French.

Marit's coral hoodie was cropped at the waist, leaving her midriff bare for nearly an inch over the waistband of her fitted white jeans.

Marit's time on the stool took mere seconds. Isabelle, on the other hand, ended up changing shoes six times before Henri was pleased with his choice.

They each went through one more change before completing their fitting.

As they left, Isabelle said, "Please tell me we're done for the day."

"Almost." Marit led her toward an elevator.

"Where are we going?"

"To pick up dresses from Ralph."

"Why?"

"For the party tonight."

Isabelle stepped into the elevator. "What party?"

"The one Lars is taking you to."

Isabelle shook her head. "I'm sorry. Why would your boyfriend take me to a party?"

"Because Lars and I were invited, and we're both allowed to bring a plus-one."

"So you're taking Cole, and Lars is taking me."

"Exactly." They reached the correct floor, and Marit headed down the hall to Ralph's office. "I told Ralph that you were coming. He agreed to loan both of us dresses."

"This reminds me of when we went to that ball in Vienna." Isabelle had enjoyed that magical night right up until Cole had pulled out his gun to question a suspect.

Marit paused in the hall. "Do you think we can get Cole to leave his gun in his hotel room?"

Not a chance. Isabelle tempered her answer. "I'm sure he'll be better behaved at this party than the last one."

Marit eyed her warily. "You aren't helping."

"Sorry." In fairness, it was the best Isabelle could offer her.

She and Marit entered the conference room, where a rack full of gowns stood against one wall.

Ralph was already there. He said something in Dutch to Marit before switching to English. Pulling a red gown off the rack, he held it up for Isabelle. "I think this is the one for you."

Isabelle moved closer to inspect the floor-length dress. A slit separated the fabric on one side, rising halfway up the thigh. Perfect for mobility. And with the right handbag, she would be able to conceal her pistol.

She glanced at Marit, who held up a pale-blue gown. Maybe Isabelle would keep her thoughts about self-defense and concealing weaponry to herself.

CHAPTER 14

Marit took Cole's arm, and they started down the pavement toward the historic Conciergerie. All along the side of the road, taxis pulled up to drop off the Fashion Week party guests. Women dressed in gowns of every description were accompanied by men in elegant and extravagant tuxedos.

"For the record," Lars said from his position beside Isabelle and behind Marit and Cole, "walking into the Conciergerie like this feels very weird."

"You're telling me," Cole said. "We're going to a fancy party in an old prison."

Marit glanced back at Lars's face and stifled a giggle. She knew exactly what Lars was feeling; she wished they were going in as a couple too. "I don't think that's what he meant, Cole," she said.

Cole frowned. "Well, it should've been. We're walking into a building with doors thicker than most walls and bars on the windows."

"And heightened security," Isabelle added as they walked past three armed police officers.

"Hopefully, that's just routine procedure at these kinds of events," Cole said. "I'm pretty sure my boss would have let me know if they were on heightened alert."

Marit eyed him warily. Was there any particular reason why that would be an issue for Cole tonight? "Heightened alert or not, you know they're not going to let you in if you brought a weapon, right?"

"You'd think so, wouldn't you?"

"Cole," Marit pressed. "We're not redoing what happened in Vienna."

"No, we're not. That time, we were flushing out a bad guy; this time, we're getting to know people."

For some reason, Marit didn't feel the slightest bit better. "Isabelle"—she turned her head—"he's your boyfriend. Talk some sense into him."

"Sorry, Marit. He's yours for the night. But if it's any consolation, I've learned it's better not to fight it."

Cole offered her a half smile. "Isabelle's right."

"That's a big ask," Lars muttered. "Your track record at these kinds of events isn't stellar."

"Don't stress over it," Cole said. "I've got this."

They'd almost reached the security checkpoint at the main doors. Marit's chest tightened. How many of these people would recognize her when her "date" set off the alarms with his concealed weapon? Even if the number was only one, word would reach Esmee and Ralph in no time, and when it hit social media, things would go from bad to worse. No one in the fashion industry wanted scandal—especially when the eyes of the world were on them.

Marit gave her and Cole's names to the woman who was checking in guests, and Cole stepped up to the metal detector. Bracing herself for the worst, Marit watched as he pulled something out of his inside pocket and showed it to the nearest officer. The officer studied it for a moment and then waved Cole around the equipment. Barely believing what she'd seen, Marit walked through the detector and met him on the other side.

"How did you do that?" she whispered.

"I have the right credentials."

"And you couldn't have told me that before I almost had a heart attack?"

He grinned. "Where's the fun in that?"

"Remind me again why Isabelle puts up with you?"

"It's one of the great mysteries of the universe," Cole said, leading her down a set of stone stairs and into a room labeled The Hall of the Men-at-Arms. "And I've decided it's best not to ask her."

Notwithstanding the anxiety he'd just put her through, Marit couldn't help but laugh. On that subject, at least, Cole was using his head. "What about Isabelle? Does she have your other gun with her?"

"No. I'm carrying both tonight. I'll pass it to her if we think she'll need it."

"Wow!" Lars said as he and Isabelle joined them. "This isn't exactly how I envisioned the inside of a prison."

Marit took a moment to appreciate the sight before them. The large room was built completely of stone. The flagstones on the floor were polished smooth. Stone walls rose to meet an elaborate network of gothic arches that were further supported by rows of marble pillars. Lights surrounded each pillar, illuminating the beauty of the ceiling above. Ornamental trees, tall urns, and elaborate flower displays had been tastefully added to the vast room, but the biggest splashes of color came from the clothing its current occupants wore.

Most people stood conversing in small groups. A few were wandering the room with a glass in hand, while others remained on the fringes, silently watching the interactions of others.

"What's the plan?" Lars asked quietly.

"We mingle as couples," Cole said. "Make note of any subtle rivalries, jealousies, or contentions between the designers. Watch for anything that seems out of the ordinary—no matter how insignificant."

"And try the food," Lars added.

"If you want to," Cole said. "The platter that just went by looked suspiciously like frog legs."

Lars pulled a face, and Isabelle laughed.

"Don't tell me frog legs rank up there with spinach, Lars," she said.

"If they don't have decent hors d'oeuvres and pastries on any of those platters, we're going out to eat when this is over," he warned.

"Deal," Cole said. "How about we meet back here in about an hour?"

With nods of agreement, Lars and Isabelle headed off across the room. Cole led Marit in the other direction. A couple passed them. Marit acknowledged them with a smile. She recognized the male model.

"Explain to me why so many designers equate weirdness with skill," Cole said.

Marit raised an amused eyebrow. "You don't appreciate a dress made of tulle filled with artificial flowers?" she asked, describing the nearby woman's gown.

"Nope. And I like my tuxes solid black, not half black-and-white stripes, half red-and-white checkered."

She chuckled softly. "I don't know. Maybe they think the crazier the design, the more vivid their imaginations."

"I think it's more like: the crazier the design, the crazier the designer."

"There may be some truth to that," Marit said, sobering slightly. "A lot of designers are a bit eccentric."

"Ralph seems like a pretty level-headed guy."

"He is. He's also brilliant. Somehow, he takes a familiar look and makes it appear completely new." She glanced at him. "Which is why the tuxes you and Lars are wearing appear both classic and original at the same time."

"And why you and Isabelle look so stunning."

She smiled. "That red gown really does look good on her, doesn't it?"

"Yeah." Cole's gaze darted to the other side of the room, and Marit caught the slight softening in his eyes when they landed on Isabelle. "Amazing."

Marit's smile widened. If Isabelle ever wanted further proof that Cole's feelings for her were deepening every day, he'd just handed it to Marit.

A server carrying a platter filled with crystal goblets cut across Cole's line of vision, snapping his attention back to Marit and the job at hand. "Ralph's over there on the left, talking to a handful of people, so let's start with a designer who doesn't seem to be so chummy."

"How about three at once?" Marit said. "I see Giuseppe Bianchi talking to Camille Allard and Kyle Adams. They're standing two pillars away from us."

"The Italian with three of his four former wives suing him for more alimony, the Frenchwoman who just took out yet another multimillion-euro loan because her last two lines aren't bringing in enough to keep her business solvent, and the American desperate to make a big mark on European fashions," Cole muttered. "Sounds like a good place to start."

Marit stared at him. "How do you know all those things?" She really shouldn't be surprised. The fact that Cole hadn't even needed her to point out which of the three designers was which simply proved his ability to access any number of sources.

"You and Isabelle have been busy with castings and fittings." He shrugged. "Lars and I had to keep ourselves occupied somehow."

"So, Lars is going into this with some background information too?" she asked.

"Yep." He placed his hand on her elbow and gently steered her toward the three designers. "It seemed like a good idea to have a basic knowledge of who we're dealing with. Especially if one of them is desperate enough to commit intellectual-property theft and murder."

Marit released a tense breath. Cole's blunt appraisal was a good reminder of why they were here.

It was time to make some introductions.

"Bonsoir, Mademoiselle Allard," she greeted her in French. "Mr. Adams. Signore Bianchi. It's nice to see you again."

"Mademoiselle Jansen." Camille Allard smiled. "You look lovely tonight."

"Thank you." Switching to English, she introduced Cole. "This is my friend, Cole Bridger. Cole, these are three of the top clothing designers in the world."

"Nice to meet you," Cole said, shaking the designers' hands in turn. "Marit has told me a little about your work. I'm very impressed."

Given their conversation of a few minutes ago, Cole's compliment was pushing it a bit, but with their inflated egos fully intact, Marit was quite sure none of them would consider him anything but completely sincere. She was proven right when each one accepted the praise without comment—as if it were due to them.

"What do you do for a living, Mr. Bridger?" Camille Allard asked.

"I'm a member of the US Diplomatic Corps," Cole said.

Allard eyed Cole's clothing and raised a critical eyebrow. "Forgive me for being impolite, but I confess, I'm surprised to see an American whose job it is to represent his country coming to this event in a Dutch designer's tuxedo."

Cole inclined his head. "You make a valid point, mademoiselle. Unfortunately, I neglected to bring my favorite Tom Ford tux with me to Paris, and when Marit invited me to attend this evening's party with her, her countryman was gracious enough to allow me to wear one of his."

Kyle grunted. "Makes sense. Molenaar's not one to turn down any opportunity to showcase his designs."

"I've seen several people wearing your clothing line this evening, Mr. Adams," Marit said. "The red-checkered suit coat is particularly eye-catching."

The American designer accepted the praise with a small shrug. "That's what it's all about, isn't it? Creating clothing that rises above mediocrity."

"Indeed." Giuseppe Bianchi joined the conversation for the first time. He raked his gaze up and down the length of her. "And to that end, Miss Jansen, as delightful as Molenaar's light-blue gown looks on you, might I suggest that next time, you choose a gown that hides less of your attractive figure."

Marit struggled to suppress a shudder. Nothing had changed since the last time she'd spoken to the unsavory Italian. He still gave her the creeps.

Cole set a reassuring hand on her back, the twitching muscle in his jaw the only indication that Bianchi's comment had infuriated him. "You obviously have a very different approach to your work than Molenaar does, Bianchi, and as someone who knows very little about the industry, I'd be interested to hear your thoughts on his current line."

Bianchi sniffed. "The man has no vision for anything that has not already been done."

"That's a little harsh, Giuseppe," Camille Allard said. "He has a remarkable eye for color. The shade of blue he chose for Miss Jansen's gown cannot be faulted."

"His use of color is good, but he lacks the bravery to combine them in a unique way. Look at Peter Wade's fabrics this year. Brilliant splashes of every hue imaginable," Bianchi said.

Marit and Isabelle had worked Peter Wade's rehearsal. The shirt Marit had modeled had been a new twist on the old tie-dye effect. The flowing trousers Isabelle had worn had made it appear as though she'd fallen into an assortment of paint cans.

"Is Peter Wade here?" Cole asked.

"Yes. He's over there, talking to Molenaar." Kyle gestured to the small group standing a few meters away, his lips curving into a mocking smile. "Maybe they're discussing the use of colors."

"Whatever they're discussing," Camille Allard said, "it will not last long."

"Why's that?" Cole asked.

"Because only a saint could put up with Peter's forceful opinions for more than five minutes." She took a sip of the sparkling liquid in her glass. "Molenaar may be a decent designer, but he's not reached sainthood yet."

"Maybe we should go and rescue him," Marit suggested.

"Great idea," Cole said, seizing the out Marit had offered. "I still need to thank him for the loan."

"Good luck to you," Camille Allard said.

"And reach out next time you need a tux," Kyle added. "I can set you up with an American one."

A server walked by. Bianchi drained his glass in time to exchange it for a full one and raise it at Cole and Marit.

Grateful she didn't have to spend any more time with him, Marit forced a smile. "Enjoy the rest of your evening," she said.

Cole took her elbow, and they moved away. "Nice people," he said dryly.

Marit grimaced. "That was a solid reminder of why I'll never work for Giuseppe Bianchi."

"Yeah. It's not hard to see why his former wives are suing him. Maybe I should double-check to see if there's anyone else he's already paid off."

"And in the meantime, you'd better gear up for a heavy dose of English arrogance."

"Arrogance, I can handle," Cole said. "A discussion on colors may be a bigger issue."

"Really?"

"I learned the 'Rainbow Colors Song' on *Sesame Street* when I was a kid. That's about as much as I've got."

With a soft laugh, Marit tucked her hand under his arm. "It's a start. And I'll back you up if the conversation veers into heathers, neons, and tertiaries."

Cole gave her an alarmed look. "If those are real words, then you'd better."

"Can someone please explain to me why they never have pizza at the parties of the high-and-mighty?" Lars said, leaning back in his chair with a satisfied sigh. "They could serve anything they want, and they choose to have snails, frog legs, and fish eggs."

Marit eyed the large white serviette she'd insisted he tuck under his shirt collar. "Maybe because they don't want to risk the guests dripping marinara sauce on multi-thousand-euro outfits."

Lars glanced downward. As far as he could tell, the serviette was still spotless. "The risk is totally worth it."

"For you and Cole, maybe," Isabelle said from her position across the restaurant table. "But Marit and I have worked with these designers. We have a better feel for how they're going to react if their loaned-out tuxes come back stained."

"So eat carefully," Cole warned.

Lars pointed at the red smudge on the serviette covering Cole's tux. "Right back at you."

Marit shook her head, worry evident in her beautiful eyes. "Seriously, guys, I know you were hungry, but coming to a pizza place in these clothes probably wasn't the smartest idea."

"Since we're not allowed in your flat, it was this or our tiny hotel room," Cole said. "We needed somewhere to debrief that was far enough from the Conciergerie that we wouldn't run the risk of being overheard by someone who was there."

Isabelle looked around. The only other customers were four casually dressed teenagers and an older man wearing the uniform of a Metro official. "I think you're safe."

"Good," Cole said. "What did you learn besides the fact that Marit deserves a medal for working with these people?"

Marit managed a small smile. "They're not all as difficult to work with as Bianchi or Wade."

"That's true," Isabelle said. "Lars and I talked to a handful who were really quite pleasant."

"What about the ones who might have an axe to grind?" Cole asked.

Lars exchanged a look with Isabelle. "Do you want to tell him, or shall I?"

"Tell me what?" Cole asked.

Isabelle sighed. "Henri LaRue had nothing good to say about Ralph. He recognized me from rehearsals and was quite put out that I'd chosen to wear a Molenaar gown rather than a LaRue gown. He threatened to pull me from his show because of my poor judgment."

"Are you serious?" Marit asked, her eyes wide. "That's terrible."

"It was a bit awkward," Lars said. "But Isabelle took it all in stride. She didn't even seem concerned."

Isabelle laughed. "Oh, I was concerned. I didn't want to be pulled from that show. It's the one right before Molenaar's. But when you've calmed irate businessmen who've come to the bank to blame a cashier for a perceived error as many times as I have, you learn to roll with the misplaced anger."

"She was pretty amazing," Lars said. "By the time we moved on, not only had she placated him, but he'd told her all about his worry that Molenaar's line was taking more than its fair share of the media's attention."

"Nice work." Cole leaned over to brush a soft kiss on Isabelle's cheek. "One designer conquered and a possible motive unearthed."

"What about Li Du?" Marit asked. "Did you talk to him too?"

"We did." Lars put his arm around Marit and pulled her closer. As much as he'd appreciated working with Isabelle at the party, he'd missed being with Marit. "His English is sketchy, and my Chinese is nonexistent, so it wasn't a very productive conversation, but when we brought up the names of his competitors, he nodded and said, 'Very good work' to every single one of them."

"He's probably one of the humblest big-name designers," Marit said.

"Okay," Cole said thoughtfully. "It sounds like LaRue bears watching, along with Allard, Adams, Bianchi, and Wade."

"What did you find with that group?" Isabelle asked.

Cole reviewed his and Marit's experience with the designers they'd spoken with. His account of Bianchi's distasteful comments made Lars fume.

"I'm sorry you had to put up with that," he said softly.

"It was over before it really began," she said. "I know to keep my distance from Bianchi." She turned her head to smile at him. "Thanks for caring."

"Always." Lars pressed a gentle kiss to her lips, a familiar thrill of attraction quickening his pulse. It was probably a good thing he hadn't been there. He'd have taken a swing at the disrespectful idiot. And it wouldn't have mattered what Bianchi was wearing; it would have ended up drenched in whatever he'd been drinking.

"It sounds like it would be worth looking more carefully at Bianchi," Isabelle said.

"I agree." Cole pulled out his phone and began entering something. "But the others aren't off the hook yet either."

CHAPTER 15

Cole waited until Marit and Isabelle walked into the building where they would rehearse for the Peter Wade show for the next several hours. His heart went out to both of them. That man really was obnoxious with a capital *O*.

Cole glanced at Lars, who stood beside him. "You ready?"

"Where are we going?" Lars asked.

"To see Giuseppe Bianchi's ex-wives," Cole said. "I need you to be my lookout."

"Why are we visiting Bianchi's ex-wives?" Lars asked skeptically.

"Because there isn't anyone better to dish dirt than a former spouse or significant other."

"Sometimes, I really worry about how you know this kind of stuff." Lars narrowed his eyes. "Isn't Bianchi Italian?"

"Yeah." Cole lifted his hand to flag down a cab.

"If you tell me we're flying to Rome, I'm going to have to put my foot down."

"Relax. We only have to go down the block. Three of his four ex-wives are here for Fashion Week."

"They're staying in the same place?"

"One is at the same place Bianchi always stays at. Apparently, ex number two's family is a part-owner of the hotel." Cole waited until a taxi stopped in front of them, and he climbed inside.

Lars took the seat beside him. "Don't you think that's a bit weird, an ex-wife staying at the same place as the ex-husband?"

"Very weird." Cole gave their destination to the driver before turning his attention back to Lars.

"Where are the other ex-wives staying?"

"They're both at hotels on the same block as Bianchi and ex number two."

"And the weirdness continues." Lars shook his head. "What makes you think they'll talk to you?"

"Because they're going to think I can help them." Cole didn't particularly look forward to deceiving the three women, but he needed information, and he needed to identify the person behind the theft of Molenaar's designs before the thief had a chance to pass them off as his or her own. Based on what he had witnessed at the party last night and in Bianchi's bank accounts, the Italian designer topped his list of potential suspects.

"What exactly do you want me to do while you're interrogating the ex-wives?" Lars asked.

"Just make sure Bianchi doesn't show up."

"Sounds like I'm getting the easy job," Lars said. "I doubt these women are going to lay out all of Bianchi's secrets for a complete stranger."

"I won't be a complete stranger," Cole said. "I'll be posing as a private investigator."

"If these women are suing Bianchi, they've probably already hired private investigators."

"I know, but I doubt the other PIs know where Bianchi is hiding his money."

"And you do?"

"Oh yeah." Thanks to a contact at CIA headquarters.

The drive to the hotel took five minutes. When they arrived, Cole led the way inside. They had to go only as far as the hotel restaurant to find Viviana Bianchi, ex-wife number two. The dark-haired beauty sat at a table in the center of the room, a waiter standing a short distance away, as though prepared to cater to her every need. Viviana appeared to be a few years older than Cole, maybe early thirties, but if her physique was any indication, she worked out regularly to fight any outward appearance of aging. Her short skirt and fitted top suggested that she shared her ex-husband's taste in fashion.

"There's one of them." Cole nodded in Viviana's direction.

"How did you know she would be here?"

"Because her hotel bill for the last three days showed her eating here at this time." Cole glanced at the nearly empty lobby. "Keep an eye out for Bianchi. Call me if he shows up."

"You got it." Lars headed for a nearby seating area and lowered himself into a plush chair facing the door.

As soon as Lars was settled, Cole crossed to the woman's table. "Viviana Bianchi?"

She lifted her gaze. "*Sì?*"

"Do you mind if I join you?" Cole asked.

"Who are you?"

"A friend of Tomasso Ricci," Cole said, supplying the name of the woman's current private investigator. "He thought we might be able to help each other."

"How so?"

Cole lowered his voice. "I have a few questions about your ex-husband, and I also have some information that might be helpful in your current lawsuit against him."

The woman's expressive eyes darkened. "Such as?" she asked, her Italian accent tinting her words spoken in English.

Cole took her question as an invitation and sat beside her. "I believe I can help you locate Giuseppe's extra funds."

Suspicion colored her words. "What do you want for this information?"

"I just want to ask you a few questions."

"And you said Tomasso sent you?" she asked warily.

"That's right," Cole lied. "When we found out our cases intersected, I offered to help you if you're willing to help me."

She tilted her head as though waiting for him to begin.

"How much do you know about your ex-husband's business?" Cole asked.

"I know everything. I met him while working as a model and ultimately managed most of his business affairs until after the divorce."

Which explained why she was suing Bianchi for a larger monthly alimony payment as well as partial ownership of his company.

"Does Giuseppe create all his designs, or does he hire young designers to help with each year's line?"

"He has other designers, but he directs everything. He has a very particular style," Viviana said. "No one at Fashion Week can quite compare."

Cole hadn't personally seen the man's clothing line, but he'd heard enough from Lars, Marit, and Isabelle to know Bianchi's line tended toward plunging necklines and high hemlines. He'd also heard that Bianchi had trouble keeping his hands to himself when it came to his models.

"Do you think he's likely to make any changes to his style this year?"

Viviana barked out a short laugh. "Never."

"How is his relationship with the other designers who are in Paris right now?"

"He tolerates them, but Giuseppe is confident in his ability to be unique."

That was consistent with what Lars had told him.

"Who would he consider his biggest competition?"

"The one he speaks about the most is Peter Wade." Viviana waved her manicured hand as she spoke the name. "But that may be because he is so difficult to work with."

"Thank you for your time." Cole stood.

"You said you have information for me."

Cole slid the banking information across the table. "If anyone asks, you don't know where this came from."

"I don't know where this came from," she said. "I don't even know your name."

"You don't need to know it." Cole left the table and headed for the lobby.

Lars joined him. "Did she give you any good information?"

"Yes, but nothing that points at Giuseppe Bianchi as the possible thief. It sounds like everyone would know if he used designs that didn't belong to him."

"After seeing what he's planning to put on the runway this year, I would agree with that. He is unique, but not in a good way."

"Let's talk to the other exes."

"Do you know where to find them?"

"Yes. Wife number three should be in the gym right about now. Her hotel is next door."

"I doubt Bianchi is going to show up at a hotel that isn't his."

"I agree, but I'd like some warning if we're wrong."

"Act as a lookout," Lars said. "Got it."

"Thanks." Cole put his hand on his cousin's shoulder. "I'll try to make this quick."

"That would be appreciated. I'd like to get back to Marit's rehearsal before too much of the day has passed."

"I think we can make that happen." Cole headed for the elevator. One ex-wife down. Two to go.

Isabelle slid into the taxi and wiggled her toes inside her canvas tennis shoes. "I never want to wear heels again."

Marit gave the driver their address and leaned her head back against the headrest. "Sorry, but you're going to have to put a pair on first thing tomorrow. We only have two more days of rehearsals before the first show."

"I don't know how you're doing all this. Or how I ended up in six shows. This is insane."

"What can I say? You're a natural."

Isabelle cast a look at Marit. "I think it's more accurate to say you're a good teacher."

"If you didn't have a look the designers wanted, it wouldn't matter how many modeling lessons I gave you," Marit said. "If Esmee has her way, this won't be your only foray into modeling."

"That's sweet, but I don't think I'm cut out for this." Isabelle glanced out the window at the Eiffel Tower in the distance, the lights already illuminated in the darkening sky. "I'm just glad Ralph's show will be my last."

"I only have two beyond that," Marit said. "And neither of them starts rehearsals for a couple more days."

Chanel and Dior had both cast Marit to walk in their shows, but those events wouldn't occur until the last day of Fashion Week. By then, Isabelle hoped to have all thoughts of modeling and runway work behind her, despite Esmee's hopes to the contrary.

"I don't know how you're going to do eight shows."

"Well I plan to sleep for three days straight after this is over," Marit said.

"I may do the same thing. I told my boss I was taking off until the Monday after Fashion Week is over."

Marit straightened and shifted in her seat to face Isabelle. "I really can't thank you enough for being here."

"Aside from the aching feet and having Peter Wade barking orders at me, it's been fun."

"Peter Wade is not known for his patience."

"That doesn't surprise me." The cab pulled up to the curb a short distance past their building, and Isabelle pulled her wallet from her purse to pay the driver.

"You don't have to pay the driver. I can get that."

"It's fine. You paid the last time," Isabelle said.

"Well, thank you." Marit stepped from the cab and shifted her bag onto her shoulder.

Isabelle climbed out and barely closed the door before the taxi driver pulled away. She slid her wallet next to the gun she had concealed inside her purse. A shadow of movement caught her attention only a second before a man stepped in front of them, his face covered by a ski mask and a knife gripped in his hand.

Marit yelped in surprise. Isabelle took an instinctive step back and slid her hand into her purse, her fingers feeling for the rubber grip of her pistol.

"Give me your bags." The man spoke in French and thrust the knife toward Marit.

Marit also had the good sense to step back. She held her hands out to the side. "We don't want any trouble."

"Hand it over." He reached his free hand out to take her purse.

Isabelle's evaluation of their potential mugger took mere seconds. The solid grip on the knife, the steady hand reaching for Marit's bag. This man wasn't new to crime, and he was far too comfortable with a knife.

She also wasn't buying the idea that Marit had been randomly targeted twice in one week.

Isabelle put her left hand on Marit's shoulder to draw her farther from the mugger, then plunged her hand into her purse and got a firm grip on her gun. "Why us?"

"Just hand over your bags." He waved the knife in front of them.

"I don't think so." Isabelle dropped her purse at the same time she pulled her gun and stepped in front of Marit. "Drop the knife."

The mugger's gaze lowered to the pistol, surprise flashing in his eyes. Then he turned and ran, darting into a nearby alley.

Isabelle lowered her weapon and glanced behind her at Marit. "Are you okay?"

Marit shook her head. "Not really."

"Come on. Let's get inside." Isabelle engaged the safety and slid her gun back into her bag. "We need to call the guys and let them know what happened."

"Twice in one week," Marit said, her words echoing Isabelle's thoughts. "Why me?"

"I don't know, but it's time we start those self-defense lessons we talked about." Isabelle opened the door and waited for Marit to walk inside ahead of her. "It will be my thank-you for teaching me how to model."

Marit held up her trembling hand. "I need to stop shaking first."

"With what I'm going to teach you, it won't matter if you're shaking or not." Isabelle headed for the lift. "Trust me."

CHAPTER 16

Marit was still trembling when she and Isabelle reached the flat. Allowing Isabelle to unlock the door and go inside ahead of her, Marit attempted to get a grip on her emotions. She didn't want to think that she was being targeted, but two muggings in less than a week made it difficult to believe otherwise. And that realization was terrifying.

"It's all clear," Isabelle called. "Come on in."

Marit walked into the living room and dropped her purse on the sofa. "These attacks are happening because of my supposed involvement in the robbery, aren't they?"

"Probably," Isabelle said, not bothering to hide her concern. "Everything started happening after Ralph's designs were stolen." She paced across the kitchen floor. "Your flat and James's room were ransacked. The thief was looking for something. James was killed in the process, but we don't know if he gave the thief what he wanted." She paused. "If he didn't, they may still think you have it."

"Have *what*?" Marit asked.

"I wish I knew." She began pacing again. "What exactly did Cole say the culprit stole from Ralph's safe?"

"The muslin patterns and a jump drive."

Isabelle stopped midstride. Pivoting, she crossed the distance between them in a few short steps. "The jump drive," she said. "It has to be." She picked up Marit's purse. "How would you feel about me dumping this?"

Marit met her eyes, a pit opening in her stomach. "If you don't, I will."

It was all the invitation Isabelle needed. She tipped Marit's purse over the sofa. Marit's phone and wallet landed on the cushion first. A cascade of smaller items rained down on top of them.

"Is there anything you don't recognize?" Isabelle asked, lowering the empty purse to the floor again.

"Yes." The feeling in Marit's stomach went from gaping emptiness to churning nausea. She reached for the black jump drive sitting on top of a package of tissues. "This isn't mine."

"Your purse was with you when the thief came to the flat," Isabelle said. "Somehow, he guessed the jump drive was in it."

"How?" Marit's hands were trembling again. She set the jump drive on the nearby coffee table and backed away from it. "*I* didn't even know it was there."

"James must have been more quick-fingered than we gave him credit for." Isabelle pulled her phone from her purse. "We need to tell the guys about this, and I think we'd better watch the surveillance video of you and James at Ralph's office again. We may not understand why James passed the jump drive off to you, but now that we know what we're looking for, we might catch something everyone missed before."

Isabelle put her phone on speaker, and the sound of ringing filled the room.

"Hey," Cole said, answering on the third ring. "Does this mean you and Marit are back at the flat?"

"Yes," Isabelle said. "We took a taxi, like you suggested, but there was a bit of an incident when we got here."

In an instant, Cole's tone switched from friendly to concerned. "What kind of incident?"

Marit sat down, the items that had been in her purse rolling haphazardly across the cushion. She didn't want to relive the moment the masked man had waved a knife at her, but she was going to have to. Probably more than once. Isabelle glanced at her.

Marit swallowed. "You tell him."

"Marit?" Cole must have heard her. "What's going on?"

Isabelle took a breath. "Some guy went after Marit again. This time with a knife. He wanted her purse, but he ran off when I pulled my gun. After we got into the flat, we started wondering why Marit's purse was the target of both attacks. We dumped it out and found a jump drive in it that isn't hers."

Cole muttered something under his breath. "We'll be right over," he said.

"You're not allowed in, remember?"

"That hasn't stopped me before. And once Lars hears what's happened, there'll be no keeping him out either."

Marit pressed her unsteady hands together. Maybe if she pretended she was okay, she'd feel more like it. "You don't need to do that, Cole," she said. "We can come to you."

"We're not going to let some thug stop us from living our lives," Isabelle added. "But I think it would be a good idea to modify our plans. Instead of going out to dinner, would you be okay picking something up? You can text me when you're back at your hotel, and we'll join you there."

Food was the last thing Marit wanted right now, but even in her upended state, she acknowledged that the others needed to eat.

"Lars and I can definitely take care of dinner," Cole said, confirming Marit's thoughts. "And I'll text you when we're back. But I don't want you walking over here alone. Especially if you're planning on bringing the flash drive with you. We'll meet you outside your building's front doors."

"That would be great," Isabelle said. "Thanks."

"I'll be in touch soon," he said. And then he disconnected the call.

Isabelle lowered her phone and gave Marit an understanding look. "I know you're feeling pretty shaky right now, but you know what will make you feel better, right?"

"Having Lars hold me for a while," Marit guessed.

Isabelle smiled. "That'll probably go a long way toward helping, but so will your first self-defense lesson." She reached for her hand and pulled her off the sofa. "Come on. We probably have thirty minutes before the guys get back. You can learn several moves in that amount of time. And if you pick them up as quickly as I think you will, you can go to bed tonight knowing that you'll get the best of the next guy who threatens you."

The image of Isabelle facing down a man with a knife wouldn't leave Cole's head. And poor Marit. A purse snatcher was bad enough, but no one should have to face an armed mugger. At least Isabelle had gone through training with the CIA to learn how to deal with such situations. Not that Marit and Lars knew that.

Cole strode down the sidewalk, a takeaway bag from a local café gripped in one hand. "I never should have let Isabelle and Marit take a taxi on their own."

"If Bianchi's third wife had been where we thought she was, it wouldn't have taken us all day to track her down," Lars said.

Cole glanced at him. The concern and guilt on his cousin's face matched his own.

"I can't believe we decided to talk to the exes on Maribelle Bianchi's spa day." Cole cringed when the vision of the sharp-tongued woman in a far-too-thin silk robe crowded his mind. "Next time, we're waiting outside the spa to ask questions."

"I don't plan on there being a next time for me." Lars pulled out his cell phone as they approached the entrance to Marit and Isabelle's building. He hit the Call button and put his phone to his ear. "We're outside." After a brief exchange, Lars hung up. "Marit said they'll be right down."

Cole handed the takeaway bag to Lars even though Lars already had a bag of his own tucked into the crook of his arm. "Here. You carry this one too. I need my hands free."

Lars didn't argue. He took the second bag.

Only two minutes passed before Isabelle came outside just in front of Marit. Both women took a good look around before continuing onto the sidewalk.

Lars immediately set the bags on the ground and pulled Marit into his arms. He held her tightly, and for a moment, neither of them spoke. "I love you," he murmured. "I'm so relieved he didn't hurt you."

"Me too." Marit's voice was strained. "It's a good thing Isabelle was there."

Cole did another quick analysis of their surroundings to make sure Marit didn't experience a third attack before he drew Isabelle into his arms to prove to himself that she was okay as well. He held her close for a brief moment before he released her. "I'm glad you're both okay."

"Me too," Isabelle said, her voice low.

Cole glanced at Marit, noting that she was carrying nothing. Smart. But he wanted her off the street regardless.

Lars drew back, his focus still on Marit. "You're sure you're all right?"

"Just a little shaky."

"That's understandable." Lars shifted so he was at Marit's side, his arm protectively around her shoulders.

Cole put his hand on Isabelle's waist and gestured across the street. "Let's get to the hotel."

Isabelle began walking. Lars released Marit long enough to pick up the food bags but stayed right beside her as they crossed the road. Cole fell in behind Marit and Lars, shielding them until they walked inside and reached the elevator.

As soon as the doors slid closed, Isabelle stepped beside Cole.

Unable to resist any longer, Cole leaned in for a brief kiss. "I'm sorry I wasn't there to pick you up today."

"It's not your fault." Isabelle lifted her hand and rested it on his shoulder. "You couldn't have known someone would be waiting for us when we got here."

"We've been trying to protect against that possibility the whole time we've been here," Cole reminded her.

"Which is why I've been with Marit at every fitting, rehearsal, and casting call."

She had a point, but he didn't have to like that she had been forced to deal with the situation on her own.

They reached their floor.

Cole and Isabelle stepped out of the elevator. Even though the hall was empty, Cole motioned for the others to go in front of them.

Lars unlocked their room. After he'd set the food down on the little table, he put a protective arm around Marit.

"You and Marit can take the chairs at the table, Lars," Isabelle said. "Cole and I can sit on the bed."

Once they were seated, Marit reached into her pocket and produced a black flash drive. "This is what we think the mugger was after."

Cole took the offering and moved to the hotel safe to retrieve his laptop.

"You know," Marit said, "if you and Lars had been with us, the mugger might not have come after us, and we might not have ever known this was in my bag."

"I guess that's one way to look for a silver lining." Cole set his laptop on the bed and plugged the flash drive into it. "I don't recognize this file type."

"May I see?" Marit stood.

Cole angled the laptop toward her.

"Those are design files. You'd need the correct program to open them."

"I don't need to open them." Cole copied the files to his laptop before he unplugged the flash drive. "If that's what is on this, the likelihood is that this is what was stolen from Ralph. All we have to do is return it to him and notify the police that it was recovered." Relieved, he held the flash drive up. "As soon as we do that, this will finally be over."

"I'm afraid it's not that simple." Marit sat back down. "As long as the muslin patterns remain out there, someone else can still copy Ralph's designs."

"But wouldn't the file prove that they're his?" Isabelle asked.

"It would help his case, but if he tries to showcase his line after someone else features the same designs in an earlier show, the public will assume Ralph is the copycat. Even if the models who tried on his clothes during rehearsals back him up, the damage to Ralph's image will be done."

Lars shook his head. "That's so unfair."

Isabelle opened one of the takeout bags and began setting out their food. "Did you find out anything new today?"

"We talked to Bianchi's ex-wives." Cole retrieved a water bottle from one of the bags and twisted the top off. "They all said basically the same thing: Bianchi has his own style."

"They're not wrong," Marit muttered.

Cole grimaced. "His exes still wear his clothes. They also insist that it would be obvious if he made a change to a more conservative approach and that Bianchi would never make that kind of switch."

Marit pushed her meal away, and Cole did not miss the slight tremble in her fingers. Still too shaken to eat. It wasn't surprising, but the realization did nothing to assuage his frustration that someone had gotten that close to her again.

"So, you don't think he's the one behind the theft?" Marit asked.

"No."

"I was kind of hoping he was guilty," Isabelle said. "Is that bad?"

"That's honest." Cole closed his laptop and secured both it and the flash drive in the hotel safe. He returned to sit beside Isabelle on the bed, noting that neither she nor Lars was eating either.

"Who do we focus on next?" Marit asked. "We're running out of time."

"We'll keep working our way through the designers based on who has shows first," Cole said.

"And we'll keep watching for anything suspicious," Isabelle said.

"Maybe I should spend some more time at your rehearsals." Lars's arm was still firmly around Marit. "The access badge Coster gave me is a press pass, so that will get me into most places."

"That's not a bad idea," Cole said. "I have a few things to take care of, and I'll feel better if Isabelle and Marit aren't alone."

Isabelle raised an eyebrow. "You know I can handle myself, right?"

Cole held up his free hand. "I never said you couldn't, but there's safety in numbers." He nodded toward the safe. "Even after we give the flash drive back to Ralph, the thief won't know Marit doesn't have it anymore."

"Which is why I gave her a few self-defense pointers," Isabelle said.

Cole wasn't sure what to say to that. Self-defense classes were great, but often, the best defense was avoiding a bad situation in the first place. And having someone who gained a false sense of confidence after learning a few moves was never a good thing. He rose to his feet. "Okay, Marit. Show me what you've got."

Marit looked at Cole uncertainly.

"Go ahead," Isabelle said. "It will be good to see how you do against someone Cole's size."

"Or I can just make sure I'm always with you or Cole, assuming the two of you keep carrying guns."

"You've got this," Isabelle encouraged.

Though Lars looked skeptical, he motioned to Cole. "My cousin gave you permission to beat up on him. You should take advantage of the opportunity."

"I'd rather not beat up on anyone," Marit said.

"You can't think that way when you perceive a threat." Cole moved to the open space of the room at the end of the bed, hoping this distraction would help Marit's mindset. "It's you or him."

"Okay." Marit approached. "What do you want me to do?"

"Let's start by pretending I'm an attacker coming at you from behind." Cole twirled his finger so she would turn around.

Marit took a deep breath and did so.

Not giving her a chance to prepare, Cole grabbed Marit around the waist with one hand and hooked his other arm around her throat.

Marit gasped. Then as though she did so all the time, her foot stomped on his, and she thrust her elbow into his ribs.

Cole's hold loosened, and Marit elbowed him again.

Cole stumbled back a step and dropped onto the edge of the bed, stunned.

"Oh, Cole!" Marit rushed forward and put her hand on his shoulder. "I'm so sorry!"

Cole rubbed at his ribs. He looked up at Isabelle's face, her expression caught between disbelief and laughter.

"Looks like Isabelle and Marit are both good teachers." Cole drew a deep breath. "But you know what they say."

"What?" Marit asked.

Cole rubbed his ribs again. "Practice makes perfect."

CHAPTER 17

LARS FLASHED HIS PRESS ID at the security guard standing at the entrance of the rented warehouse. With a nod, the guard waved him through, and Lars walked inside. A temporary catwalk had been set up in the center of the large space. On one end of the runway, large curtains cordoned off the portion of the room being used by the models; on the other end, a cluster of photographers was gathered behind a row of tripods and cameras.

Sliding the strap of his camera case more securely onto his shoulder, Lars moved toward the group of photographers standing behind their tripods, waiting for Camille Allard's rehearsal to begin. When he spotted Tony, he smiled. The English photographer had been more than eager to engage in conversation at Ralph's rehearsal. If Lars were lucky, a few well-placed questions this morning might lead to some useful information.

"Hey, Tony," Lars greeted the older man.

"Lars! Nice of you to join us." Tony shifted to his left to make room for Lars. "I heard Molenaar helped Allard out last year, but I didn't know he went as far as sharing the Coster jewelry with her."

Lars blinked, scarcely believing his luck. Tony had tossed out that valuable nugget of information before he'd even formulated a leading question. Tamping down his impatience to know more, he shook his head. "No shared jewelry. I just know that on the day of Molenaar's show, I won't get many chances for the right shot. The more practice I have with the models on the runway, the more confident I'll feel in the moment."

"Makes sense," Tony said. "If we told people how many photos we take before we get the winning shot, they wouldn't believe us."

"Right?" Lars unscrewed the legs on his tripod and set it next to Tony's. "So, what can you tell me about Allard's show?"

Tony shrugged. "From what I've heard, it's classic Allard pieces. The lady's French, but she's less dramatic than most of her colleagues—with her clothing line and her temperament. I don't suppose we'll hear much shouting at this one."

Lars desperately hoped Tony's assessment proved right. After what Marit and Isabelle had gone through the night before, they could use a drama-free rehearsal.

"What did you mean when you said Molenaar and Allard have worked together in the past?" he asked.

"Well, it was a bit hush-hush," Tony admitted. "But word on the street was that Allard was forced to close her manufacturing plant for three months because of a fire."

"Whoa. That can't be a good thing for a big-name designer."

"Nope," Tony said. "And it happened a couple of months before the London shows."

"What did she do?"

"Swallowed her pride and asked for help." Tony adjusted the shutter speed on his camera. "Bianchi turned her down. No big surprise there. Some say LaRue did too. Must be that the rivalry between the two of them is stronger than their shared nationality."

"So, she approached Molenaar?"

"Or the other way round."

"Molenaar offered his help without being asked?" Lars said.

Tony shrugged. "I can't verify that, but in the industry, Molenaar's known as one of the better fellows. According to the unreliable old grapevine, Molenaar cleared his manufacturing plant of his clothes for three weeks to let Allard's team go in and produce theirs in time for the London show."

Lars released a low whistle. "I don't suppose that happens often."

"I think *never*'s the word you're looking for," Tony said. "I get that Molenaar cleared the facility of his stuff first, but in a business where most designers are looking over their shoulders to see if anyone's trying to steal their ideas, it was a generous move."

"How often do you think that actually happens?" Lars asked. "The stealing of ideas, I mean."

"Who knows. If you listen for them, there are always rumors about that kind of thing buzzing around, but it seems like nothing's ever proven." He took a seat behind his camera. "Take Peter Wade, for example. A couple of years ago, Bianchi came out swinging, claiming Wade had stolen his color palette for that year's spring line. He denied it, of course, and since Bianchi never offered any proof, his accusation eventually fizzled and died. Nobody talks about it anymore."

But that would not be the case if Bianchi had backed up his claim. Peter Wade's career in the fashion industry would have been over. Lars's thoughts flew to Ralph. No wonder the guy was desperate. If the person who'd stolen his patterns and designs produced them after accusing him of stealing, the charge would appear evidence-based. The black mark wouldn't disappear the way the one pinned on Peter Wade had.

"It's a cutthroat industry," Lars said.

"You've got that right." The stage manager appeared at the runway entrance, and Tony moved closer to his camera. "And I'm glad I'm on this end of it."

Tony was right. He and the other photographers didn't have much to lose if one of the designers went rogue, but the woman Lars loved did. Marit wouldn't be safe until they'd figured out who was behind the theft at Ralph's office and James's death. If Lars could pass on this new information about Allard to Marit while she was backstage, there was a possibility that she and Isabelle could discover the truth behind the rumors from her crew. Knowing whether Allard felt gratitude or resentment for Ralph's intervention would go a long way in determining her status on the suspect list.

Lars pulled his phone from his pocket. He flexed his fingers, attempting to work out some tension as they hovered over the keypad. The second model was already on the runway. It was possible that Marit wouldn't see his text until it was too late to act on it, but he had to at least try. Angling his phone so Tony couldn't see the screen, he typed a short message to Marit. As soon as he'd sent it, he copied it, added the tidbit about Peter Wade, and sent it to Cole. The more his cousin knew before talking to Ralph again, the better.

Releasing a tight breath, he looked up to see Marit standing at the runway entrance. At a signal from the man at the curtain, she started toward him. Lars adjusted the focus on his camera and took a few photos of her approach. When she reached the end of the runway, she stopped and smiled at the photographers. Lars lifted his phone. Marit gave no indication that she'd noticed, but Lars knew that didn't mean anything. He'd yet to meet anyone as observant as Marit. And if she'd guessed he needed her to check her phone, somehow, she'd find a way to do it.

Cole approached the security desk, the flash drive gripped firmly in his hand, the backup copy still safely on his laptop. Having the information in Cole's possession wouldn't hurt Ralph, but it would ensure that proof existed to show that Ralph had created the images if another theft occurred.

"I'm here to see Ralph Molenaar. He's expecting me." Cole picked up the pen by the sign-in log and wrote down his name.

The guard picked up the phone and glanced at Cole's name before relaying the message that Cole had arrived. As soon as he hung up, the guard said, "Do you know where his office is?"

"*Oui*," Cole said, utilizing the little bit of French he knew. "*Merci*," he added as he headed for the elevator.

When he stepped off on the correct floor, the buzz of voices carried from a nearby doorway. Several people stood by another office down the hall. A young woman emerged from Ralph's office, a garment bag draped over her arm.

Cole moved past her and knocked on Ralph's open door.

Ralph stood behind his desk, a pen in hand as he made a note on the paper in front of him. "Just a moment." He held up a finger briefly before he stopped writing and straightened. "Sorry. Everything is a bit chaotic today. Our show is just over a week away, and we're still making adjustments."

Cole closed the office door before he held out the flash drive. "I believe this is yours."

Ralph's eyes widened. "Where did you find it?"

"It was in Marit Jansen's purse." Before Ralph could jump to the wrong conclusion, he added, "We believe Brinton James planted it there after Marit caught him in your office."

"But the police never found it."

"They questioned Marit, but they never went as far as obtaining a search warrant," Cole said. "After reading the lead detective's report, I believe they eliminated her as a suspect after she provided so many specific details about the night of the theft."

Ralph lowered into his chair and held up the flash drive. With a shake of his head, he said, "And this has been in her purse ever since it was stolen?"

"Yes. We went through her bag last night after an attempted mugging." Cole sat across from Ralph and explained the sequence of events along with the unsuccessful purse snatching.

"Thank goodness Marit is okay." Ralph set the flash drive on his desk. "And having this back will help me defend myself when whoever stole my designs tries to call me a thief." He sighed. "I can only hope my adaptations will be significant enough to prevent that from happening."

"Marit said the missing patterns could still pose a significant problem."

"Very much so," Ralph said. "Only four years ago, Dominic Vitale went out of business within six months of showing the same outfit as Peter Wade at New York Fashion Week."

Suspicion hummed through Cole. "That's twice I've heard Peter Wade's name come up with regard to a potential intellectual-property theft."

"Ah, yes. The color palette from Bianchi three years ago." Ralph nodded. "That did cause quite a stir."

"Do you think Peter was guilty?"

"I don't know. He launched a line of rather revealing miniskirts that year. It's possible Bianchi was simply casting blame as a warning for him to steer clear of what Giuseppe considers his territory."

His territory. Meaning sleazy. Cole kept that thought to himself.

"Of the designers going before you, which would benefit the most from stealing your designs?" Cole motioned toward the door behind him. "Or from putting you in the position of trying to reinvent your designs so close to your show?"

"I hate to say it, but if I were forced out of business, they all would benefit."

Cole pulled out his phone and retrieved his notes app. "I know you're busy, but this is important. I need to know everything about these other designers, right down to who you think is capable of theft." Cole paused. "And murder."

CHAPTER 18

The moment Marit walked through the curtain backstage, her assistant, Sophie, was at her elbow.

"You have three minutes for this change," Sophie said, unzipping the gown Marit was wearing as she spoke.

"What about the next one?" Marit asked.

"Two," Sophie said grimly. "That one's going to be tight."

A one-minute difference between outfit changes was huge. And far too big to ignore. When she'd seen Lars raise his phone, she'd known exactly what he'd meant. She also knew that he wouldn't have signaled her during a rehearsal unless the message he had for her was important. She popped her high heels off and reached for the flats she was scheduled to wear with the loose-fitting trousers. Given half a chance, she could move fast in these.

"Quickly, Sophie," she said. "I need to grab something from my purse before I get back in line."

Sophie frowned. "What is it? With the number of buttons on this shirt, you're barely going to have time as it is."

It was now or not until the end of the rehearsal.

"My phone," she said.

With an alarmed expression, Sophie pressed her finger to her lips. "If Mademoiselle Allard catches any of us backstage on our phones, we're fired."

Brilliant. It was a common practice to silence all phones while backstage, and checking them during work hours was discouraged. But not many designers enforced a total ban on their use.

"I'm expecting a really important message," Marit said.

"More important than losing your place in the show?" Sophie asked.

"Yes." If the message had anything to do with Ralph's missing patterns, it trumped walking in Camille Allard's show.

Sophie's eyes widened. She'd obviously not expected Marit's emphatic response. She straightened Marit's collar and glanced over her shoulder. "The general manager's talking to the in-line help," she said. "Put on the jacket, and I'll go with you. If we're stopped, we're looking for a safety pin."

"Bless you, Sophie." Marit threaded her arms through the sleeves and hurried across the waiting area.

Darting into the small room where the makeup-artist stations were lined up along the wall, she ran to the row of cubicles where the models left their personal items.

One of the makeup artists looked up from clearing her desk. "Do you need something?"

"A safety pin." Marit had found her purse and was already rooting through it for her phone.

"Shouldn't your assistant have tons of those?"

"I usually do." Sophie had entered the room. The anxiety in her voice was probably due to the ruse they were undertaking, but it was exactly how a wardrobe assistant would sound if she'd truly run out of pins. "I used my last one on the first outfit."

Marit clasped her phone. Keeping it hidden inside her purse, she pressed the screen. A message from Lars. She pressed the screen again to open it. Behind her, Sophie was asking the makeup artist if she had any safety pins. Marit scanned the message.

Rumor that Ralph helped Allard out last year with clothing manufacture. Can you find out if it's true?

Letting her phone drop back into the bottom of her purse, Marit turned and ran for the door. "Got one, Sophie. Let's go."

Sophie needed no second bidding. She was right behind Marit when she reached the lineup. Isabelle was already in position, two girls from the head of the queue. She raised a questioning eyebrow, but Marit had no time to do anything but go directly to the head of the line.

The woman standing by the curtain glanced at her clipboard and frowned. "That was close, Miss Jansen. Watch for your cue."

Sophie tugged on one of her sleeves to straighten it. Seconds later, the curtain was pulled back, and Marit stepped onto the runway again.

Grateful that traversing the catwalk was virtually second nature, Marit mulled over Lars's message as she walked. She didn't know Camille Allard well enough to ask her about the rumor, so her best option was to find someone who'd worked with her for over a year. Sophie would have been an ideal candidate because clothing assistants spent a good deal of time listening to talk backstage. But she'd already told Marit that this was her first time working for Allard. Her newly hired status explained her strong motivation to keep all the designer's rules.

Marit reached the bank of photographers. Inclining her head, she smiled. The camera shutters clicked, and as she turned to go, she gave Lars a faint nod.

Sophie was waiting for her when she passed through the curtain. They exchanged only a few words, focusing instead on the clothing change. As soon as the chiffon bow was tied around her neck, Marit stepped back in line.

Isabelle appeared through the curtains. Needing to make no further changes, she headed straight for Marit. "Everything okay?" she asked softly.

Marit nodded. "I had a message from Lars." The model directly in front of her moved onto the runway. Marit didn't have time to explain. "See if you can find someone who's worked for Allard for over a year," she whispered. "I'll fill you in when I get back."

The clipboard-wielding woman called her forward. "You're up, Miss Jansen."

Sophie met Marit when she returned. "Mademoiselle Allard wants you in the first outfit for the finale," she said, already helping Marit out of her trousers.

"How long do I have?" Marit asked.

"Eight minutes."

Marit breathed a sigh of relief. With any luck, she could find Isabelle before they both went back out.

"Hi, Marit." As though Marit's thoughts had summoned her, Isabelle appeared at her elbow. "I wanted to introduce you to my assistant, Ellie. I don't know what I would have done without her today."

"Hi, Ellie," Marit said. "Do you know Sophie?"

Ellie shook her head. "I don't think we've met yet."

Sophie offered her a shy smile. "I'm new, so I don't know many people."

"I've been with Mademoiselle Allard for three years, and I still don't feel like I know people," Ellie said sympathetically.

Marit offered Isabelle a look of appreciation. It had taken her friend less than ten minutes to come through with someone who could help them.

"You must like working for Mademoiselle Allard to have stayed on so long," Marit said.

"I do." Ellie lowered her voice a fraction. "She's kinder to her workers than most designers."

"I'm glad to hear it." Marit paused. There was no easy way to bring this up, so she might as well dive right in. "Kindness tends to cycle around eventually. I did hear a rumor that Ralph Molenaar helped her out a while ago."

"He did." Ellie's brow creased. "That was a bad time for everyone in the company—especially Mademoiselle Allard. There was a fire in her manufacturing plant, and the insurance money didn't come in for months. Without a functioning plant, there was no way Mademoiselle Allard could produce her line in time for the London show without help. Monsieur Molenaar offered her the use of his facility. I don't know what Mademoiselle Allard would have done otherwise."

"Monsieur Molenaar is another kind person," Isabelle said.

"Yes. And I know Mademoiselle Allard is grateful to him. They'll always be competitors, you know, but underneath it all, they maintain a friendship and respect for each other's work." She shook her head ruefully. "You don't see that among many of the designers."

"No, you don't," Marit agreed.

"Places, ladies." The woman with the clipboard began directing all the models into the line.

"We'd better go," Marit said.

"Of course." Ellie stepped back. "Sophie and I will wait here for your return."

Marit and Isabelle moved to take their positions in line.

"Thank you," Marit whispered to Isabelle. "Ellie was exactly who we needed."

"And who Sophie needed."

"Yes." Marit smiled. She'd had the same thought. "That too."

CHAPTER 19

Isabelle leaned back against the headboard of Cole's bed, a napkin and a boxed salad on her lap, or rather a plastic container filled with lettuce and cucumber. It could hardly be considered a salad when it didn't include any toppings or salad dressing. Lars and Marit had once again opted to sit at the little table beside her, and Cole currently paced at the far end of the room, his open laptop in one hand. He was in work mode at the moment, his focus unbreakable. Why she should find him so attractive when he got like this, she couldn't say, but at the moment, she was having a hard time keeping her eyes off him.

"Cole, it will be a lot easier to look at your screen if you stop pacing," she said.

Cole simply made another turn at the edge of the room, the laptop still balanced on his hand.

Isabelle took a bite of salad. "When all this is over, I say we go out for a nice Italian dinner with lots of pasta and creamy sauces."

Marit held up her fork, which currently had a wedge of tomato attached to the end of it. "That sounds so wonderful."

"As hard as you two have been working, you deserve a little spoiling," Lars said.

Cole's focus remained on his laptop screen as he strode to the door and then back to the foot of the bed again. "From what Ralph said, we can eliminate half a dozen designers from suspicion, including Li Du and Kyle Adams. Neither of them has any sort of production abilities here in Europe, not even on a small scale."

"And if we're right about Camille Allard, she would be too grateful to Ralph for helping her out previously to ever try to sabotage him," Marit said.

"Ralph indicated the same thing to me."

"That leaves Henri LaRue and Peter Wade as our top suspects." Isabelle slid off her shoes and let them fall to the floor before pointing her toes in an effort to work out the stiffness in her arches.

Cole set the laptop down and sat at the edge of the bed, just beyond Isabelle's bare feet. "Peter's name has come up twice now as possibly being involved in thefts before." Cole nudged the laptop toward the center of the bed and took her foot in his hands. He pressed his thumb against the bottom of her foot, right in the spot where it ached the most.

Isabelle dropped her plastic fork into her salad box and sighed. "Oh, that feels good."

"It's supposed to." He continued massaging her foot. "Maybe it's time we take a closer look at Peter Wade's operation."

"What did you have in mind?" Lars asked.

Isabelle suspected she knew exactly what he had in mind. "Does Wade have offices here in Paris?"

"Yes." Marit pushed the remains of her salad back onto the table. "Including a small production studio."

Cole's gaze lifted to meet Isabelle's. He cocked both eyebrows as though asking her opinion of him breaking in without a government order behind him.

"If you do this, you'd better not get caught," she said.

"Do what?" Lars asked.

"I just want to poke around his office a bit," Cole said innocently. He really did have that look down.

"Peter Wade is not going to invite you into his office," Marit said. "And he certainly won't leave you alone to let you search for whatever might show his guilt."

"I wasn't planning to ask for an invitation." Cole released Isabelle's left foot and moved on to massage her right.

Lars's eyes widened. "You're going to break in?"

"I'm just going to take a look around."

Lars shook his head. "Please don't tell me I'll need to bail you out again."

"You didn't have to bail me out last time," Cole said. "You just gave me a ride home from the police station."

"Same thing." Lars took another bite of his sandwich, melted cheese oozing from the size of it.

Cole pressed on a particularly tight spot on the ball of Isabelle's foot, and she flexed her foot to give him better access. He was definitely winning serious brownie points right now. Despite that, Isabelle couldn't disagree with Lars. "Lars may be right on this one," she said gently. "None of us can afford to have you end up in jail right now."

Cole released her foot and stood. He moved to her side and leaned down to kiss her. His lips only touched hers for a moment, but it was enough to send the familiar warmth and love rushing through her. He leaned back and smiled. "I'm not going to get caught."

Lars set down the remains of his meal and glanced at Marit. She smiled at him, but there was no mistaking the tiredness in her eyes and the slight droop to her shoulders that spoke of the pressure she'd been under this week. He reached for her hand, anger at the person responsible for sending men to assault her rippling through him. Fashion Week was taxing enough for a model of Marit's caliber without adding an additional fear factor. Along with that, he and Marit were together in Paris, and instead of strolling hand in hand through a quaint outdoor market or spending a romantic evening at an elegant restaurant, they were holed up in a tiny hotel room, eating boxed salads. It was time to do something about it.

"Want to go somewhere new?" he asked softly.

She gave him a startled look. "Do you think we can? I'm not sure that I'm ready to test my self-defense skills on anyone but Cole."

"We can," he said firmly. "And you're going to be completely safe." He pulled her to her feet. "Put on your coat and give me one second to grab mine."

That caught Cole's attention. "Are you two going out?"

"Yes and no," Lars said, taking his coat out of the tiny closet.

"Try that again," Cole said with a frown.

"Yes, we're going outside," Lars said. "No, we're not going to be on the dark streets, where the bad guys hang out."

"Until we know who's behind the attacks on Marit, it's probably unwise to go anywhere farther than our building," Isabelle said.

"Agreed." Lars reached for Marit's hand again. "We won't leave the hotel."

Cole folded his arms. "But you're going out?"

Lars released a sigh. Given their current situation, it had been a forlorn hope that he could have any significant time alone with Marit, but he was not giving up on claiming a moment or two.

"We're going onto the hotel roof," he said. "When I was acting as your lookout at Bianchi's hotel, I noticed a sign advertising a rooftop bar, so when we got back here, I asked at the front desk to see if they have anything similar." He shrugged. "They don't. But they do have roof access, and when I told the clerk that I was a photographer and wanted to get shots of the Parisian skyline, she gave me the code to the outside door. I checked it out earlier. By daylight, it's half a dozen outdoor chairs and a small, rickety table sitting on a large patch of gray roofing material. I'm hoping that by night, it's a quiet getaway with a view of the city all lit up."

"Sounds great," Cole said, reaching for his and Isabelle's coats.

"Actually, you weren't invited."

Cole grinned. "I know. But for security's sake, I should check it out. And I'm not leaving Isabelle here on her own."

Lars gave him a long-suffering look. "I'll give you the key code on two conditions." He held up one finger. "First, the roof is to be a no-talk-of-work-or-pending-danger zone." He held up another finger. "And second, you and Isabelle must hang out far enough from me and Marit that I can pretend I'm alone with my girlfriend."

Humor shone in Cole's eyes. "On the assumption that my security sweep finds the rooftop clear, you've got yourself a deal."

It took Cole less than a minute to scour the hotel rooftop and declare it safe. "It's a bit breezy up here," he said, "but Lars was right: the views are amazing."

Taking Isabelle's hand, he led her to the far side of the building, allowing Lars and Marit to claim the corner that looked out over the Seine. Lars tucked his arm around Marit's small waist, and they moved to stand beside the wrought-iron railing that ran around the perimeter of the roof.

The wind tugged at Marit's hair, sending wisps streaming across her face. She laughed, capturing the wayward strands in one hand and tucking them into her coat. Her joy at such a small thing was the best thing Lars had witnessed all day.

"I've missed this." He drew her closer. "I've missed you."

"I've missed you too." Relaxing against him, she laid her head on his shoulder. "Thank you for finding this place and for bringing me here. It's perfect."

Her definition of *perfect* needed a little work, but Lars wasn't going to argue with her. He didn't care how dilapidated the chairs behind them appeared, or how sooty the chimney stacks were that lined the rooftop. All that mattered was that they were together and that she was happy.

"Look," she said, pointing at something far below them. "Do you see the little tour boats all lit up?"

Lars smiled. "I do."

"And the glass pyramid at the Louvre."

"Uh-huh."

She turned her head and caught him watching her. "You're not even looking at how pretty it is," she accused.

"Yes, I am." An errant strand of hair escaped her coat again, and with gentle fingers, he brushed it off her face. "And if you were to ask me, I'd say my view is stunningly beautiful."

Her expression softened. "You must like the windswept look."

He turned to face her, sliding his other arm around her waist. "I *love* the windswept look," he said. "And the fancy-party look, and the first-thing-in-the-morning look, and the I-just-took-down-Cole look . . ."

She laughed softly. "That was the stunned look."

"Whatever it was, it suited you." He sobered. "I'm sorry for all the terrible things you've had to endure this week. You've been so brave and so uncomplaining."

"You didn't see me shaking like a leaf after the last mugging attempt."

Regret coursed through him. "I wish I'd been with you."

"I would have just had you hold me." She threaded her arms around his neck. "And maybe kiss me."

He brushed his lips gently across hers. "Like this?"

"Kind of." Her fingers found his hair, and his heart began to thump.

"'Kind of' isn't good enough. Can I try again?"

Her lips were tantalizingly close, and they curved upward.

"I think maybe you'd better."

This time, when their lips met, Lars let his emotions free. Days' worth of fear and anxiety over Marit's well-being mingled with the thrill of holding her in his arms. Her fingers wove through his hair, and he tightened his hold on her as the rooftop seemed to tilt beneath his feet. The wind swirled around them, his kiss silently expressing his ever-deepening love even as he accepted hers.

From somewhere far below, a siren wailed, the sound increasing in volume as the police car drew nearer. Marit shifted slightly. Slowly, reluctantly, Lars raised his head to rest his forehead against hers. This woman was everything to him, and he couldn't imagine—didn't want to imagine—a future without her in it. He moved one hand in a slow circle across her back. It was time. As soon as he returned to Amsterdam, he was going to talk to Coster's head jewelry designer about a ring.

"Was that more like it?" he asked.

She nodded faintly. "Uh-huh."

"Pretty sure I'll remember how from now on."

"That's good," she whispered. "But if you need to practice again, that's okay too."

Lars smiled into the darkness. "More practice sounds like a great idea."

CHAPTER 20

Cole tightened the straps of his backpack and checked the back of the building yet again. A stray cat at the edge of a garbage can eyed Cole warily, the hair on its back sticking straight up as it debated whether Cole was a big enough threat to cause it to leave the scraps it had been eating when Cole first arrived.

With no other hint of movement, Cole climbed on top of the dumpster nearest the fire-escape ladder, bringing him to within three feet of the bottom rung.

Bending his knees, he jumped straight upward and grabbed the bottom rung with both hands.

His weight pulled the ladder downward with a grinding squeak. The cat scurried away, and Cole winced. He hadn't meant to make that much noise.

The ladder jolted to a stop when it was mere inches above the dumpster. He glanced around again for any sign of life before starting his upward climb. He stepped onto the first-floor landing, careful to balance his weight to avoid making more noise. He then continued up the stairs to the rooftop, six stories up. Looming above him from only a couple of kilometers away, the Eiffel Tower shone brightly. Too brightly.

Ducking to keep from being seen by anyone who might bother to look up, he continued to the edge of the building. Who was he kidding? It was two in the morning. Only crazy people were up at this hour.

Voices carried from below, and Cole peeked over the edge of the roof. A man and a woman leaned on each other as they swaggered down the street. Whether they were intoxicated or exhausted, Cole couldn't tell, nor did he care.

He climbed onto the edge of the rooftop, deliberately focusing on the four-foot gap between him and the next building instead of the six stories of empty space below him. Just like the standing long jump at field day in junior high, except for the lack of soft sand in his landing zone.

He bent his knees and swung his arms back. Then he took a deep breath and launched himself onto the next roof. He cleared the opposite ledge but stumbled as he fought to regain his footing. One hand pressed against the rooftop before he righted himself and continued to the spot above where Peter Wade's office was located on the fifth floor.

Cole evaluated the surrounding rooftop before attaching his rappelling gear to a window-washer anchor. It was a stroke of luck that he'd needed this particular equipment on his last assignment. He set his secondary line on the second window-washer anchor, along with the motor that would allow him to use a remote to pull him back up to the roof rather than forcing him to climb back up manually.

Once satisfied that his rigging was secure, he did another check of the street below. The couple had disappeared, but the hum of a nearby engine kept him in place until a car drove by and the street was once again quiet.

Planting his feet on the edge of the rooftop, he tightened his line and climbed downward. He reached the fifth floor and counted off the windows to make sure he entered the correct one. Thankfully, no light shone from within.

Cole stood on the railing of the balcony and retrieved a thin, narrow metal strip from the zippered pocket on the front of his backpack strap. Twenty seconds later, the window latch clicked open.

Cole pushed the window open and slipped inside. He remained stationary for a moment while he evaluated the space before him. A large designer's table in the corner, two stools beside it. A small, wooden desk in front of the window. A long couch pushed against the far wall.

Confident that he was alone, he pulled the end of the rope into the room and unhooked his harness. A quick scan revealed that the office was clear of surveillance cameras and motion detectors. That would simplify things.

He searched the office, beginning with the desk, which had only a single center drawer. It wasn't even locked. He slid it open to find nothing beyond basic office supplies.

The artist's table was devoid of everything except a pencil holder filled with various colored pencils and pens.

He moved to the nearest piece of artwork, a print of the Eiffel Tower. He pulled it away from the wall enough to ensure that nothing was hidden behind it. He repeated the process with two more framed prints without success.

Continuing forward, he reached the far side of the room and discovered a small niche tucked into the corner. Inside it was a four-drawer filing cabinet.

Cole picked the lock and started at the bottom drawer. Bingo. A small safe with a combination dial had been fitted inside. What was it with everyone hiding their safes in drawers?

He studied the top, unable to identify the manufacturer. That was going to complicate things. Unless . . .

Cole dialed Isabelle's number.

Isabelle answered on the third ring. "What kind of safe is it?"

"How did you know I was calling about a safe?" Cole whispered.

"Because it's . . ." She trailed off, and he could hear her sheets rustle. "Two fifteen in the morning."

"Okay, so it's about a safe, but I can't tell what kind." Cole described it.

"It's probably a Forrester," Isabelle said. "Zero first, then a four-digit combination."

"Thanks."

"Just don't get arrested."

"I'll text you when I'm on my way back."

"Thanks." Isabelle hung up, and Cole pulled out his specialized listening device.

At least this time he didn't have as tight of a time constraint as he'd had for his break-in last week. He simply needed to open the safe, find any evidence that would prove Wade was involved with the theft, and get out before he showed up in the morning—and before anyone noticed Cole's rope hanging off the side of the building.

Working steadily, Cole dialed through the combination, restarting twice when the second number gave him some trouble. Forty-two minutes later, he pulled the handle and lifted the safe door to reveal the contents inside. A bunch of beige fabric.

Could these be what had been stolen from Ralph's safe? Or had Wade created them?

Cole lifted the fabric from the safe and laid out the pieces on the couch, photographing each one in turn. When he reached the last one, he looked in the safe for anything else hidden within, but only a small stash of cash remained.

Cole returned the fabric to the safe and secured it before pulling open the next drawer to the filing cabinet. He flipped through the files, all of which appeared to be old tax records.

He closed that drawer and opened the next one. This time, the files were labeled with names rather than years. Cole took photos of each label, pausing when he reached Giuseppe Bianchi's name. Cole pulled the file out and opened it. Inside were several legal documents, including an opinion from Wade's attorney on whether to sue for defamation. Cole photographed the documents, carefully keeping them in order in the file.

He replaced it and only had to look to the one right behind it before he came to another familiar name: Dominic Vitale.

This file was much thicker and included a police report that outlined Wade's claim that Dominic Vitale had paid one of Wade's employees to steal one of his designs.

Not willing to take the time to read the entire file, Cole snapped photos of the documents and replaced them.

He finished his search of the filing cabinet without any other significant finds.

The chime of an elevator rang out. Whether it was a guard or an occupant didn't matter. Cole was out of time.

He hurried across the room as footsteps approached. The telltale jangle of keys followed.

Cole quickly clipped his harness to his primary and secondary lines and stepped out onto the railing.

The lock in Wade's door turned as Cole pulled the windows shut. Without hesitation, he hit the button to start the motor, his body lifting into the air, and he zipped upward to the roof.

The moment he reached the top of the building, he climbed over the ledge and pulled his line upward.

"That was close." He shook his head. Why would Peter Wade be in his office at three thirty in the morning?

It didn't matter. It was time to get back to his room and get some sleep.

Cole packed his gear into his backpack and headed back the way he'd come. He had just landed on the roof of the building next door when his phone buzzed with an incoming text.

He thought he had silenced it.

Based on the late hour, it had to be either his grandfather or a friend who was Stateside. Continuing steadily forward, he pulled his phone free of his pocket. He glanced down at the screen. Not a text message. An alarm.

CHAPTER 21

A STRIDENT BEEPING JOLTED MARIT awake, and she shot up in bed, her heart racing. "Isabelle!"

A door clicked. Someone coming in or going out?

Isabelle's pale shadow flitted across the bedroom, headed toward the living room. "It's one of the motion detectors," she whispered. "I'm on it. Don't move."

Don't move? While Isabelle went out there alone? Marit might be shaken, but she wasn't going to simply sit in bed and wait for her friend to be attacked.

Sliding out from under the sheets, she reached for her phone on the bedside table: 3:55 a.m. If Cole had followed through on his plan to visit Peter Wade's office, he probably wasn't even in bed, let alone asleep. He also wasn't going to answer her phone call. She pulled up Lars's number and pushed Call. It rang once before Lars picked up.

"Marit? What's wrong?"

"Someone tripped the motion sensor," she whispered, the ongoing clamorous noise filling every corner of the flat. And probably beyond.

"Where are you?"

"In the bedroom." She swallowed. "Isabelle's gone out there."

"Text Cole," he said. Over the phone, she heard a door slam and the pounding of running feet. "I was waiting up for him, but he's not back yet. I'm on my way over."

The phone went dead. A thud sounded from the living room. Marit darted across the room, pressing herself against the wall beside the open bedroom door. The whisper of fabric moving. Was it Isabelle or someone else? Marit strained her ears, trying to determine which way the person was going.

"Marit?"

At the sound of Isabelle's voice, Marit's knees weakened. "I'm by the door."

Isabelle entered the bedroom, the moonlight peeking through the chinks in the blinds and reflecting off the gun in her hand. "He's gone."

"Did you see him?"

"Yeah." Frustration filled her voice. "Black clothes, black mask. By the time I reached the front door, he was halfway down the hall. He took the stairs, and I knew I wouldn't catch him even if the elevator was waiting on our floor."

Female voices reached them from outside the flat. With a groan, Isabelle hurried over to the chest of drawers and picked up her phone. Two seconds later, the alarm shut off, and an eerie silence descended on the flat.

"I should have done that first thing," Isabelle said. "Then maybe it would have only woken us up instead of everyone on our floor."

As if to prove the point, someone banged on their door. "Marit! What's going on? Are you okay?"

"What do I tell them?" Marit asked.

"The truth." Isabelle slipped her gun beneath her pillow. "That someone tried to break into this flat. Again. We'll reassure them that the alarms scared off the perpetrator and apologize for waking them. That's all they need to know at this time of night."

Releasing a tense breath, Marit started for the door. "I don't know what happened to the security guard downstairs, but whether Esmee likes it or not, something significant is going to have to change if we're staying here another night."

Lars tore out of the hotel. At this early hour of the morning, the traffic was light, and he barely paused to look both ways before sprinting across the road. Taking the steps that led to the entrance to Marit's building two at a time, he reached for the door.

"Lars!"

He swung around. Running footsteps approached from his left, and seconds later, Cole materialized out of the shadows.

"Did Marit text you?" Lars asked, pushing open the door as he spoke.

"I haven't checked." Cole was out of breath. "I was just leaving the other place when my phone registered that the motion sensors were triggered. I've been running ever since. Have you talked to her?"

"Yeah. But that was at least two minutes ago."

Neither of them needed to be told how quickly a situation like this could change. Especially if weapons were involved.

Cole withdrew his gun and entered the empty lobby beside Lars. "The front door should have been locked. And where's the security guard?"

"I don't know, and I'm not waiting to find out." Lars made for the door bearing a sign showing stairs. "I'm not waiting for the lift either."

"Good call." Cole was right behind him. "It's so tiny, we probably couldn't fit both of us and my backpack in it anyway."

With a grunt of agreement, Lars started up the stairs. "Which floor are they on again?"

"Fourth," Cole said, glancing up the stairwell. "It looks clear, but keep your ear out for anyone coming down."

Lars took the stairs faster than he'd ever climbed stairs before. And he was reminded of how much he hated them. "This is it," he panted when they reached the fourth floor.

"Yeah." With his free hand, Cole reached for the door. "Let me go first."

Cole opened the door a fraction and peered out through the narrow opening.

"What do you see?" Lars asked.

"Three women talking in the hallway," he said.

"Is any of them Marit or Isabelle?"

"Nope," Cole said. "Try calling Marit."

Lars dialed Marit's phone.

She answered immediately. "We're both okay," she said. "The intruder bolted when the alarm went off."

Lars released a ragged breath. "Thank goodness. Where are you now?"

"In our flat. Where are you?"

"Almost in your flat," he said. "What number is it?"

"412. But—"

"We'll be right there," Lars said.

"They're okay?" Cole asked as Lars disconnected.

"Yeah. Number 412. Let's go."

Cole opened the stairwell door wide enough that he could glance up and down the hall. He held up his hand to have Lars wait. Lars tensed. What now? A door closed, and Cole's hand dropped.

"We're clear," he said. "The women who were out there just went into their flats."

Moving rapidly, the two men entered the hall. Lars glanced at the numbers on the nearest doors: 408, 409.

"Turn right," Lars said. "The numbers are going up that way."

410. 411. Another door clicked, and suddenly, Isabelle was standing in front of them. Her eyes widened, but without a word, she stepped back into the flat, leaving the door open for them to follow.

Vaguely aware of Isabelle locking the door behind them, Lars crossed the small living room in six long strides and wrapped his arms around Marit.

"You're really okay?" he asked.

She nodded, clinging to him as he pressed a kiss to her lips.

"It was a good thing we put in the motion sensors," Isabelle said. "The alarm spooked the intruder enough to send him running before he got any farther than the front door."

"Did you see him?" Cole asked.

"Yes, but not well enough to ID him."

Cole must have recognized her frustration. He brushed a kiss across her cheek. "It's okay. How long ago did he disappear?"

Isabelle glanced at the clock hanging on the wall. "About five minutes ago."

Cole nodded. "He's probably long gone—especially if he was working with someone else—but I'm going to do a quick sweep outside the building just in case." He met Lars's eyes. "Stay with the girls. I don't care who tells you that you're not allowed in here. Don't leave."

"I'm not going anywhere," Lars said, tightening his hold on Marit.

Cole nodded. "Lock the door behind me. I'll be back soon."

Isabelle opened the door again. The sound of the lift grinding its way upward filled the hall. Cole glanced that way and then took off toward the staircase in the opposite direction.

Locking the door behind him, Isabelle released an exasperated sigh. "Do we call the police, or do we assume someone else already has?"

"Is that really necessary?" Marit asked. "Other than our alarm waking everyone in the building, nothing happened."

Lars understood her reluctance. He'd lost track of how many times she'd spoken with a police officer since she'd arrived in Paris.

"It's the waking-everyone-in-the-building part that I'm worried about," Isabelle said. "It'll be a miracle if no one called in a complaint."

A knock sounded at the door.

"If Cole's back already, that's probably not a good thing," Lars murmured. "If it's the police or an irate neighbor, that isn't much better."

"Marit!" A woman's voice called through the door. "Isabelle! Are you in there?"

"It's Esmee," Marit whispered.

Esmee pounded again.

"I don't think she's going to go away." Isabelle reached for the doorknob and gave Lars a pointed look. "You'd better brace yourself for a dressing down."

"Let her in," Lars said grimly. "I have a few things she probably needs to hear too."

Isabelle opened the door. "Hi, Esmee."

Marit's agent entered, a pink silk dressing gown covering her matching pajamas. "What's going on up here?" she demanded. "Alarms. Models running around the halls in the middle of the night." She turned to look at Marit, and catching sight of Lars for the first time, she placed her hands on her hips. "And now a man in the building?"

Lars met her glare without flinching. "You forgot to mention the thug who got past the supposedly vigilant security guard and just broke into Marit and Isabelle's flat. Again."

Esmee turned shocked eyes on Isabelle. "Is this true?"

"Yes," Isabelle said. "After the first break-in, Cole insisted that we put a motion sensor at the door, and it's a good thing we did. The alarm went off when someone entered our flat. Thankfully, that was enough to scare him away."

"I called Lars, and he came right over," Marit said.

"You should have called the police," Esmee said even as the faint wail of a siren entered the flat.

"It sounds like someone else did that," Lars said.

Esmee clutched the lapels of her nightgown. "This is terrible."

"Yeah, it is," Lars said. "And so, from tonight on, either you find Marit and Isabelle somewhere else to stay, where Cole and I can keep them safe, or you break your no-men-allowed rule, and let us camp out in this living room."

"It would be impossible to find alternative accommodations in this part of the city with Fashion Week's opening in two days," Esmee said.

"Then we go with the other option," Lars said. "Cole and I are well used to sleeping on sofas."

"I cannot allow—"

"You don't understand," Lars interrupted her. "We already tried your solution, and it failed. Who knows where the security guard was just now. And whatever new locks the locksmith put on didn't do the job either. If that guy tries to get to Marit and Isabelle again, he's going to have to go through me and Cole."

For the first time, Esmee's expression showed a hint of indecision. "But the other models. What do I tell them?"

"That they're safer with Cole and Lars staying in the building than they would be if the men weren't here," Marit said.

"And if they request that their boyfriends come too?"

"Tell them you are making an exception only because Cole and Lars have experience with security matters," Isabelle said.

Under those conditions, Cole certainly qualified. It might be stretching the truth a bit in Lars's case, but if practice watching security feed counted, few people could match him.

"I won't lie to them," Esmee said.

"It wouldn't be a lie," Isabelle said.

Esmee was vacillating. Lars could sense it. Maybe a reminder of what she stood to lose would be helpful. "There is a third alternative," he said. "If you don't think Cole and I can keep them safe, Marit and Isabelle could leave Paris. I'm sure you agree it's not worth risking their lives to stay here unprotected."

Esmee's eyes flashed with something that looked remarkably like panic. "I'll speak to the building supervisor," she said. "You can stay until the police have taken care of the threat. But only until then."

A phone rang in her dressing gown pocket. Esmee pulled it out, frowned, and answered it. "This is Esmee." She paused, listening intently to whoever was on the other end. "Yes. I understand. Thank you for telling me." She hung up. "Well, it looks like I won't have to speak to the supervisor until later this morning," she said. "That was the security guard downstairs. It seems that he returned to the lobby from the men's room to discover the police sealing the building. No one is to go in or out until they've determined what happened." She offered Marit a regretful look. "They're on their way up."

"I'll go into the hall with Esmee to meet them," Isabelle said. "Will you let Cole know what's happening?"

The moment Isabelle and Esmee walked out, Lars pulled out his phone and called Cole. The phone rang four times before his cousin answered it.

"What's going on?" Cole asked.

"The police are here and have sealed the building," Lars said.

"Yeah, I guessed that might happen when I heard the sirens. Have they reached the girls' flat yet?"

"They're on their way up."

"Okay," Cole said. "I should be there in just a minute."

"The police won't let you—"

"Hey, would you have Marit go stand at her bedroom window?" Cole said as though he hadn't even heard Lars. "I want to make sure I have the right one."

Lars lowered his phone. "Cole wants you to go stand at your bedroom window."

Marit gave him a puzzled look but hurried into the room behind her. Moments later, there was a slight thud. Lars arrived at the open bedroom door in time to see Cole appear outside the glass. Marit yanked the window open, and Cole slid inside. As soon as his feet were firmly on the floor, he released the harness he was wearing.

"Thanks for opening the window," Cole said. "That made things a lot easier."

Lars stared at him. "You rappelled in here from the roof?"

Cole shrugged. "I already had all the equipment with me, and I knew where the fire escape was." He looked at Lars's face and chuckled. "I told you I'd only be a minute."

Lars rolled his eyes. "You get to explain to Esmee how you got in here."

"Esmee's here?"

"She and Isabelle went into the hall to meet the police," Marit said.

Cole stuffed his harness into his backpack and tossed his jacket onto a nearby chair. "I'll go join them. If Esmee asks where I was earlier, we'll tell her I was in the bathroom."

"Okay," Lars said. "But for the record, the security guard downstairs already used that excuse."

CHAPTER 22

Isabelle stood between Esmee and Gardien Chalamet as the police officer explained that he would remain in the building until morning.

"Do you have any idea what happened to the extra guard the building manager hired?" Isabelle asked.

"They only had him working until they locked the building down at night," Gardien Chalamet said.

"They assumed no one could get past the locked doors?" Isabelle asked with a shake of her head.

The apartment door opened behind her, and Cole stepped into the hall.

"This is all so disconcerting." Esmee folded her arms tightly, her entire body tense. "First, Marit being taken in to talk to the police, then the attempted muggings, and now this."

"I'm clearly missing some information." Gardien Chalamet furrowed his brow. "And where did you come from?"

Cole ignored the officer's question and pulled out his cell phone. "I can give you the case numbers for the first three incidents."

Not sure what cover Cole would use with the officers and not wanting to subject him to Esmee's watchful eye, Isabelle wrapped her arm around Esmee. "Esmee, I'm sure Gardien Chalamet and Cole have this under control. Why don't I walk you back to your apartment?" Esmee opened her mouth as if to object. Isabelle pushed on before she had the chance. "With the first show starting in two days, you need your rest. It won't do for you to have bags under your eyes at the last day of rehearsals while you're representing so many feature models."

"I suppose you're right."

Isabelle gently guided Esmee to the elevator. The doors slid open, and Isabelle intended to follow her inside, but Esmee stepped in and held her hand up.

"I can make it from here. You need to get some sleep too." Esmee motioned to Cole. "And tell your boyfriends to behave and stay out of sight. I don't need backlash from the other girls."

"I'll pass along your message." And she would. She just didn't know if Cole would heed it. He was in safety-first mode, and she doubted that he or Lars cared much about appearances after what had happened.

Isabelle waited until the elevator doors slid closed with Esmee inside before returning to Cole's side.

"Anything you can get us on those cases would be appreciated." Cole retrieved his credentials from his pocket and showed them to Gardien Chalamet. "The last update I received on the murder case said only that they didn't have any new leads."

"I agree that these are all related, especially in light of the jump drive found in Miss Jansen's bag," Gardien Chalamet said, his concern obvious.

"And unless the thief knows Marit no longer has it, she'll continue to be in danger."

"With how much we've adjusted the security around her, we've narrowed down the possible locations where her bag could be stolen," Isabelle said.

"That's true," Cole said, considering. "We're escorting you to and from rehearsals and fittings, and we're adding another layer of security here at your flat."

"Right. The only place the thief could really get to it now is backstage during one of our rehearsals or during a show, if he could manage to get back there."

Cole's eyes lit with understanding. "We need to set up surveillance in case someone tries."

"Exactly," Isabelle said.

Gardien Chalamet nodded. "We can assign a female officer to stand nearby to watch for anyone who might search Miss Jansen's bag."

Isabelle considered the chaos of the backstage area. "As easy as that sounds, I'm not sure you would be able to plant an outsider without her being noticed," Isabelle said. "It's crazy busy backstage, but it's an organized chaos. Once you get through rehearsals, everyone pretty much knows who belongs."

"Setting a trap won't work unless someone is there to witness it snap shut," Gardien Chalamet said. "Assuming the thief can get back there in the first place."

"Since whoever is behind this is clearly an insider in the industry, it's only a matter of time before someone goes for the purse backstage," Isabelle said.

"Lars and I could go backstage," Cole suggested.

"You're outsiders too," Gardien Chalamet said.

"Lars isn't," Isabelle said. "He's been at several rehearsals taking photos. And a lot of people have seen Cole hanging around as well."

"Two men backstage where women are dressing will be noticed," Gardien Chalamet said.

"Marit can make a point of leaving her bag in one of the cubbies closest to the makeup stations," Isabelle suggested. "That area is largely deserted during the show, and I can set up a couple of hidden cameras."

"Your officers can monitor the cameras, and you can always plant an officer or two in the audience," Cole said.

"We will already have officers standing by outside for crowd control," Gardien Chalamet said, "but I doubt we'll have the manpower to put someone on watching surveillance images."

"We could always plant a tracker inside the purse," Isabelle suggested.

"That's not a bad idea, but we really need to catch our thief in the act," Cole said. He focused once more on Gardien Chalamet. "Any chance you can get us a couple of backstage passes?"

Gardien Chalamet seemed to ponder the possibilities. Finally, he shook his head. "I doubt it. Not without tipping someone off about why we want them." He lowered his voice a fraction. "Your best bet for that may be to use your embassy resources."

Or Agency resources. The French policeman had no idea what Cole's contacts were capable of doing. And the fact that Isabelle had a backstage pass they could copy only made things easier.

Gardien Chalamet reached into his shirt pocket and produced a business card. He handed it to Cole. "Call me if you have any further information."

Cole nodded. "One more thing: Can you turn off the alarm for the door to the roof for about five minutes once you get downstairs?"

"Why?"

"I left something up there that I'd rather not leave unattended at night."

"I'll do that as soon as I get downstairs. Text me your number so I can let you know when it's clear."

"Thanks."

Isabelle waited until the officer retreated down the hall before she asked, "Your rappelling gear?"

"Yeah. I don't want to give our intruder an easy way in." Cole texted Gardien Chalamet and slid his cell into his pocket.

Isabelle took his hand in hers. "Thanks for coming."

Cole laced their fingers together. "I'm sorry I was late."

"You're here now." She pushed onto her toes and pressed her lips to his.

She had expected the kiss to be brief, a simple affirmation that Cole was here and they were both safe, but Cole drew her closer, and the adrenaline from the past twenty minutes poured into the kiss. Suddenly unbalanced, she settled her hands on his shoulders as one kiss led to another.

The rattle of water running through old pipes sounded overhead, and women's voices carried in muted tones from a nearby apartment. All of that faded beneath the sensation of the bubble she and Cole had created in this moment.

Isabelle's pulse quickened as Cole drew her closer. Her love swelled inside her, the words expressing her feelings demanding an escape. She fought against the urge to share the depth of her love. Cole was still adjusting to having a girlfriend. Moving toward something that could bring permanence to their relationship could very well send him into panic mode.

His phone buzzed, interrupting the private moment. Cole pulled back. "Sorry. That's probably Gardien Chalamet."

"It's okay. Go get your stuff. I'll meet you inside."

Cole nodded and leaned forward for one more kiss, his lips lingering on hers as though he didn't want the kiss to end.

Warmed by the gesture, she waited for him to disappear into the stairwell before she headed inside.

Marit and Lars were sitting on the couch, Lars's arm firmly around Marit, when Isabelle walked in.

Marit lifted her head from his shoulder. "Is everything okay now?"

"Yes. Gardien Chalamet will stay in the lobby tonight." Isabelle closed the door behind her. "Cole is running up to the roof to grab the gear he left up there."

"Until I met Cole, I thought living on an upper floor was safe," Marit said.

"Living on an upper floor is never safe." Lars used his free hand to rub his thigh. "All those stairs can be a killer."

"Which is why you should never live somewhere without a lift," Marit teased.

Grateful that their moods seemed to have settled, Isabelle retreated to her room and retrieved her backstage passes for the various shows. She laid them out on the kitchen table and used her phone to photograph them, front and back.

"What are you doing?" Marit asked.

"Helping Cole so he can get some backstage passes made for him and Lars."

"Why?" Lars asked. "I already have a press pass."

"I know, but we have a plan." Isabelle proceeded to explain the backstage surveillance they had discussed with Gardien Chalamet.

"That's a great idea," Lars said.

"I'd better clean that bag out to make sure there's nothing in it that I don't mind losing in case it does get stolen," Marit said.

"We can stage it so it looks like you're really using that bag, but instead, we'll have your stuff in mine."

"We need to get you a bigger bag," Marit said.

"I bet Esmee can help me with that."

"Or Ralph," Lars suggested. "I'm sure lending Isabelle a bag is a small sacrifice for identifying the thief."

"That's true."

A knock sounded at the door, and Cole walked in before Isabelle could cross to it. He closed and bolted the door behind him.

"How did your investigative work go tonight?" Marit asked.

"Actually, I need your help to answer that." Cole pulled out his cell phone, unlocked his screen, and passed it to Marit. "I found these inside Peter Wade's safe."

Marit's eyebrows lifted. "You broke into his safe?"

Sidestepping her question, Cole asked, "Can you tell if those are Wade's or Molenaar's?"

Marit scrolled through the images, zooming in on each one. "Those are Peter's designs."

"How can you tell?" Isabelle asked.

"Two things." Marit held up the phone so Isabelle and Cole could see it. "Peter puts his initials on the bottom of each pattern."

"Couldn't he have done that after he stole Ralph's designs?" Cole asked.

"Maybe, assuming Ralph doesn't put a marking on his, too, but this pattern here is for the dress I'm wearing in Peter's show. I tried it on before Ralph's patterns were stolen."

Lars sighed. "I was really hoping it was him."

"Me too, but only so this would all be over," Marit said.

"We've narrowed down the field a lot," Cole said. "If you keep scrolling, you'll see the documents I copied."

Marit's eyes widened. "He was suing Bianchi?"

"He thought about it." Cole grabbed a kitchen chair and straddled it. Leaning his arms on the back of it, he continued. "Wade had a case, both for theft and for defamation, but his attorney advised him against it. Looks like he's been the victim of corporate espionage a time or two."

"So, where does this leave us?" Isabelle asked.

"By my count, we only have one solid suspect left." The blue of Cole's eyes darkened. "Henri LaRue."

CHAPTER 23

Early morning light filtered through the curtains, the flat quiet except for the water running in the bathroom. Judging by the number of times the shower had turned on and off, everyone had now taken a turn. Of course, Cole had taken his turn at five in the morning. Once the police lock-down had lifted, he'd made a quick trip to his hotel room to retrieve his and Lars's belongings.

Cole stretched his legs out on the couch, where he'd slept a couple short hours, and balanced his laptop on his thighs. Even though the second bedroom had two twin beds, he hadn't been willing to leave the living area empty, not with someone so determined to get to the flash drive.

With a clear suspect in mind, Cole searched through the updated police reports for anything that could lead back to Henri LaRue or someone associated with him. Unfortunately, not only did the files contain nothing helpful, but nothing new had been added in days beyond a mention that the four incidents were likely related.

He straightened when he noticed an additional incident that had been attached as well. He clicked on the link, grateful that his current access allowed him to do so without having to hack his way in. He skimmed over the initial report, leaning forward as he did so. Another murder. The victim appeared to be a small-time criminal, in and out of jail over the past decade, but the ballistics matched the weapon used to kill James.

The shower turned off, the pipes rattling when it did so. Then footsteps retreated into one of the bedrooms.

Lars emerged a few minutes later, his hair damp. "I assume our intruder didn't try to come back again last night."

"No." Cole closed the police reports and opened a secure portal into the CIA's database. "There is a new development in the police reports though."

"What's that?" Lars opened the refrigerator.

"Another man was killed by the same gun that killed Brinton James."

Lars slowly closed the fridge, and his gaze met Cole's. "You mean by the same person who killed Brinton James."

"Most likely."

"Who was the victim?"

"His name is Pascal Bernard. Based on his photo and his rap sheet, it could be the guy who tried to steal Marit's purse on Friday. If that's the case, LaRue could be trying to tie up loose ends by eliminating potential witnesses against him." Cole turned his attention back to his screen.

"Any chance you can prove Henri LaRue is behind all this?" Lars asked.

"I'm still looking." Cole located the email address for Henri LaRue and opened a new tab on his secure internet browser. He accessed the email server LaRue used, which was conveniently tied to his website. Hacking through the encryptions took only a few minutes. "Here we go."

"What?" Lars asked.

"Henri LaRue's calendar is tied to his email account."

"Any chance there's something in there about breaking in last night?"

"I suspect he's using hired hands for that sort of thing," Cole said. "The people he hired are only important if they can point a finger at who hired them, assuming they live long enough to share that information."

"I don't suppose his calendar shows any meetings between him and his hired thugs," Lars said hopefully.

"No, but I do know where he's going to be at nine thirty this morning." Cole looked up at Lars and wiggled his eyebrows. "And you're going to like it."

"Where?"

"He's meeting his business manager for breakfast," Cole said. "I say we go out to eat after we drop the girls off at rehearsal."

"I could go for some real food."

Isabelle and Marit emerged from the short hallway. Both of them wore breezy silk blouses and blazers over dress pants. Their makeup was understated but still enhanced their features. Cole rather liked Isabelle with those dark lashes framing her incredible green eyes.

Isabelle crossed the room and sat beside him on the couch. "What are you two plotting?"

"Breakfast."

"Do not tempt me with pastries this morning," Isabelle warned. "I have no willpower after eating like a model for the past few days."

"Don't worry. We aren't going out until after we drop you two off at your rehearsal." Cole pointed at the calendar displayed on his screen. "Lars and I have a breakfast date."

Marit stepped beside Lars and rested her hand on his shoulder. "Would you two mind dropping by Ralph's offices today to see if Isabelle can borrow a handbag?"

"We'll take care of it," Cole said, "but only if you promise not to go out on your own."

"We'll be at rehearsals all day," Marit said. "They're even bringing in lunch for us."

Isabelle wrinkled her nose. "I'm not sure I want to know what they think constitutes a meal."

"Good luck with that." Cole leaned over and kissed her cheek.

Marit pulled two yogurts from the refrigerator and handed one to Isabelle along with a spoon. "You should eat something. We need to leave in ten minutes."

Isabelle took the offering and peeled off the foil wrapper on top. "If Cole and Lars can prove LaRue is behind the theft and the murder, does that mean I can quit the modeling thing before Fashion Week starts?"

"It's too late for that," Marit said. "Esmee would never forgive either of us if you backed out now that we've gone through all the rehearsals."

Isabelle's face paled. "How did I get myself into this?"

"You were the only one who could pass for a model and also stay with Marit," Cole said. "Remember?"

"You and Lars are staying here now."

"Yeah, but Marit didn't turn us into models." Cole stood and held up his laptop. "I did want you to look at something before we go." He pulled up the image of the latest murder victim on his laptop screen. "Have you ever seen this guy?"

"That's the mugger." Isabelle leaned closer, her surprise evident. "He's dead?"

"What?" Marit hurried across the room and looked over Isabelle's shoulder. "What happened?"

"Best guess is that whoever hired him to steal your purse decided to make sure he couldn't talk."

"That's terrible," Marit said.

"And scary," Isabelle added.

"I'm sure the police will let us know when they have any new leads," Cole said, hoping to alleviate everyone's concerns. Of course, if the police were really interested in keeping them informed, they would have told Cole about the new murder case instead of just giving him access to the reports. He might not have even noticed had he not kept checking for updates.

Pushing that irritation aside, he headed for the door. "Come on. We need to get you and Marit dropped off so we can get to the restaurant early."

"Walking around in high heels or sitting at a restaurant eating real food." Isabelle scowled. "I'm definitely getting the short end of this stick."

The restaurant was small, the signage elegant and upscale. Urns filled with greenery stood on either side of the smoked-glass front doors, and the outdoor seating was enclosed by a stylish railing.

Lars glanced at the menu posted at the entrance and gave Cole an uncertain look. "You sure about this? Have you seen these prices?"

"I can guess," Cole said. "But if an exorbitant breakfast helps us pin the theft at Ralph's office and James's death on LaRue, it's worth it."

There was no arguing with that, especially since Marit's safety was directly connected to taking into custody the mastermind behind the crimes.

"Besides," Cole continued. "Worse comes to worst, you could order one croissant. That probably wouldn't break the bank."

Given the prices he'd seen, Lars wasn't so sure. "Are you telling me that you have the self-control to eat only one croissant for breakfast?"

"I didn't say that was *my* plan. But you can make it yours if you want." Cole grinned. "You'll just have to eat it really slowly because we need to stay long enough to overhear what LaRue and his business manager have to say."

Lars glanced at the restaurant doors. "How's that going to work exactly?"

"We're resorting to old-fashioned eavesdropping. Or you are anyway. They'll probably be speaking in French, so I'm going to need you to translate for me."

"And how do you plan to get us close enough to hear what they're saying? Places like this don't have open seating. We're going to be taken to a table."

"Yeah, I know," Cole said. "But I bet they take requests."

"You're going to request to sit next to LaRue?" Lars asked.

"Not in so many words." Cole pulled open the door and lowered his voice. "As soon as we're inside, scour the room. You know what LaRue looks like. Once you've spotted him, we'll ask for the table beside him. I'll walk in front of you so he doesn't get a good look at you. Take the chair that puts your back to him."

"*Bonjour*!" A young woman approached them with a smile.

"*Bonjour*," Cole said. "Do you speak English?"

It would have been just as easy for Lars to talk to the hostess in French, but Cole was obviously buying him time to scan the occupants of the restaurant.

"Of course." She smiled politely. "Welcome to Café Eugenie. May I show you to a table?"

The restaurant was busy, but there was no sign of LaRue anywhere in the room. Lars and Cole had purposely arrived five minutes after the designer's appointment to ensure that he'd already be seated.

"That would be great," Cole said. "Do you have a preference for where we sit, Lars?"

Lars skimmed the room again, and this time, he spotted a narrow wooden staircase in the corner that appeared to lead up to another floor. Perhaps this restaurant wasn't quite as small as it had appeared from the outside.

"Do you have more seating upstairs?" he asked. "Something a little more private maybe?"

The hostess smiled. "The upper room is a favorite with our regular customers, but I believe there are still a few tables available." She picked up a couple of menus. "If you'd follow me, please."

They followed her across the polished wood floor and up the narrow staircase. She waited for them at the top.

"You're in luck," she said. "There's a vacant table beside the window."

For a restaurant with such an exclusive ambiance, it undoubtedly was lucky. And under normal circumstances, Lars would have been happy to sit there. But this wasn't a normal day, and LaRue was sitting at a small table in the far corner, talking animatedly to an older man with silver hair and wire-rimmed glasses.

"Actually," Lars said, "would you mind if we took the table over there in the corner?" The fact that the table next to the one LaRue was using was also vacant was taking their luck to the next level. Lars could only hope it would remain in their favor.

The hostess offered him a polite, albeit surprised look. "Certainly."

"He's heard so much about the food here, he doesn't want anything—including a view—to distract him," Cole said.

Their hostess laughed lightly. "That I can understand. We French take our food very seriously. And I'm confident our chef will not disappoint."

Cole stepped in front of Lars as they walked across the room, blocking him from the view of the other men. Cole took the chair facing LaRue, leaving Lars to take the one that backed up against the designer's business manager. The space was tight, but Lars slid onto the seat without giving the older gentleman reason to adjust his chair or glance his way.

Their hostess handed them the menus. "Jean will be your server today," she said. "And he'll be with you momentarily."

"*Merci*," Cole said.

Lars managed a nod and a smile. He was already focused on the intense conversation going on behind him.

"Fournier has given us his ultimatum, Henri." The business manager was speaking. "If he does not see anything that excites him in this year's show, he'll offer your retail space to a different designer."

"He can't do that," LaRue said. "We have a contract."

"It ends in August," his business manager reminded him. "Which would be just right for someone else's fall line to make an appearance."

"It won't happen."

Lars wasn't sure whether to categorize LaRue's tone as belligerent or alarmed. Perhaps both.

"Fournier may think he knows what's coming, but he's in for a surprise."

Lars tensed, cocking his head slightly so as not to miss a word. All he needed now was for LaRue to let his business manager in on what that surprise was—a fresh new line that closely resembled Molenaar's style—and they'd have the proof they needed.

"*Bonjour*!" A man dressed in a white shirt, a black tie, and black trousers stepped up to the table.

Lars glanced at the menu. He hadn't even opened it yet.

Cole took one look at him and spoke to the server in English. "I'd like this omelet." Cole pointed to something on the menu. "Along with a glass of orange juice and a croissant."

"Very good." The man—Jean, presumably—turned to Lars.

LaRue was saying something, and Lars couldn't concentrate on both conversations. "Whatever he's having would be great," he said.

Jean inclined his head politely. "Of course."

"Better make it a basket of croissants," Cole said, amending his order.

"*Oui, monsieur*." Jean gathered the menus, and Lars returned his attention to the conversation behind him. To Lars's frustration, LaRue was speaking again. Whatever clarification he'd offered his business manager regarding the surprise at his show had been lost during the breakfast order. Lars frowned, and Cole raised an expectant eyebrow.

"What's going on?" Cole asked softly.

Lars shook his head. Any explanation would have to wait until after he'd listened to the demands LaRue was now issuing.

"It's less than a week before the show, so make sure Fournier has a front-row seat. If he's after clothing that will suit any shape or size, he'll be both pleased and impressed. It won't matter whether he's trying to appeal to the wealthy customers at his boutique on the Champs-Élysées or to those who buy off the rack in Lyon; he should see what he wants to see."

"I certainly hope so." LaRue's business manager sounded grim. "You can't afford to lose that account, Henri. Without it, the bank will offer you no more concessions—or money."

Jean approached, a hot pot of coffee in his hand. He stopped at LaRue's table, and for a moment, the only sound was the trickle of liquid being poured into a cup.

"May I get anything else for you, gentlemen?" Jean asked.

"No, thank you," LaRue replied.

Jean walked away, and the light clink of a spoon hitting against the sides of a china cup filled the silence. Lars waited. Cole studied him, his curiosity simmering. Finally, LaRue spoke again.

"The show will generate the excitement we need," he said. "You will see. And now, on to other things. Tell me what news you have from Delhi. Can they provide the cotton we need?"

As LaRue's business manager launched into the details of an agreement with a cotton manufacturer in India, Lars leaned over the table.

"It doesn't sound like things are looking good for our friend," he muttered. "An awful lot is riding on the upcoming show."

Speculation shone in Cole's eyes, but before he could ask anything, Jean appeared at the table, carrying a large tray.

"Your juice and croissants," he said, placing a glass of orange juice in front of each of them before setting a basket of fragrant croissants in the center of the small table. "And your omelets."

Lars leaned back, and Jean set a plate in front of him. The fluffy omelet was enormous. Cheese oozed from its center, and flecks of orange, red, and green ran along its outer edge.

"This looks great," Cole said. "Thank you."

"My pleasure." Jean gave a pleased smile. "May I get you anything else?"

"Not right now, thanks," Cole said.

Jean nodded and walked away.

Lars looked up from his study of the omelet. "What kind of omelet did you order?"

"Vegetable and brie." Cole reached for a croissant and set it on his plate beside the egg.

"It has spinach in it," Lars accused.

"Yep." Cole shrugged. "Isabelle's rubbing off on me."

"You know how I feel about spinach."

Cole grinned and took a bite of his croissant. "Next time, you might want to ask what I've ordered before getting the same thing."

Lars glared at him. "I was slightly preoccupied. Besides, I thought you had my back."

"I do." He pointed to the basket. "See? I ordered way more than one croissant."

Marit stood beside Lars, holding his hand as they waited for Cole to open the door to the flat and for him and Isabelle to enter ahead of them.

"Okay," Cole called a few seconds later. "Come on in."

"One day, I'll be able to enter my flat without worrying whether someone else has gone in before me, right?" Marit asked. After a full day of rehearsals, it was a challenge to keep the weariness out of her voice.

"Yes," Lars said firmly. "And if Cole and I have anything to do with it, that 'one day' will be very soon."

She waited until he'd closed the door behind them. "Did you learn anything at the restaurant?"

"Enough to know that LaRue is in a pretty tight spot financially, and his new line needs to be really well-received if he's going to make it out intact."

"Did he say anything about Ralph's designs?" Isabelle asked, setting her purse on the floor and entering the conversation as she dropped onto the sofa.

"Not directly," Lars said. "But he talked about surprising people with his designs at the show."

Cole sat next to Isabelle and put his arm across her shoulders. "I wish he'd given away more, but he said enough to keep him at the top of our suspect list."

"I wish that meant I could skip working all the other shows but his." Isabelle took off her shoes and grimaced. "I'm not sure what I'm most worried about: messing up in front of an army of photographers or destroying my feet forever."

"I'm afraid blisters come with the job," Marit said, rooting through her purse for her container of plasters. "Here." She handed them to Isabelle. "I've been modeling so long my feet have become calloused. I don't get nearly as many blisters as I used to, but I still keep these on hand."

"What are they?" Cole asked.

Isabelle showed him the small box. "Stretchy Band-Aids."

He gave her a sympathetic look. "How about you put those on and then I give you a foot rub? I can avoid any areas that are covered."

Isabelle leaned toward him and kissed his cheek. "You're the best," she whispered.

Lars drew Marit into his arms. "What are the chances that I would get a kiss if I offered to rub your feet?"

Laughing softly, Marit slid her arms around his neck. "High. So, so high." She looked up at him, her heartbeat quickening at the look in his eyes. "Although, you might get one just for walking me home from rehearsal this evening."

"I was kind of hoping you'd say that," he said.

"You were, huh?"

"Absolutely." Without another word, he lowered his lips to hers, and for several seconds, she lost herself in the wonder of loving this man—of being loved by him.

Then Cole's voice reached her from the sofa.

"Seriously, guys?"

Reluctantly, she drew back. Lars continued to hold her, the moment they'd shared lingering even though they could not call back the kiss.

"And here I thought his tricking me into eating spinach this morning was bad," Lars muttered.

Marit smiled. "You ate spinach?"

"Half a leaf, at most," Cole said. "He left the rest on the side of the plate."

Isabelle looked from Cole to Lars. "Was this at the fancy restaurant you went to for brunch?"

"Yeah," Lars said. "And the spinach tasted the same as it always does. It was just more expensive."

Isabelle laughed. "What else did you learn while you were there?"

"Not much more than we've already told you," Cole said. "LaRue and his business manager left soon after we got our food. I called the police once they were gone to check on the James and Bernard investigations." He frowned. "No new leads."

"So, what do we do now?" Marit asked.

"Well, since Fashion Week officially starts tomorrow morning, Lars and I will walk you and Isabelle to the Carrousel du Louvre for Camille Allard's show," Cole said. "While you're working, we'll see if we can find anything of interest backstage."

"Is there anything we should be working on tonight?" she asked.

Cole looked at Isabelle and raised an eyebrow. "What do you think? Some last-minute modeling lessons for you, or another self-defense session for Marit?"

"If Marit's feeling half as wiped out as me, we both need to spend at least half an hour doing nothing more than scrolling mindlessly through YouTube videos on our phones."

Marit laughed. "That sounds amazing."

"Right?" Isabelle gave Cole a deceptively innocent look. "Although I'm pretty sure holding a mug of hot chocolate in the other hand would make it even better."

Cole chuckled. "Am I going out for this hot chocolate, or is there some in the kitchenette?"

"Try the cupboard to the right of the sink," Marit said.

Cole crossed to the cupboard, opened it, and pulled out a box. "Do you want some, too, Lars?"

"Sure."

"Great." Cole opened another cupboard. "Four mugs of hot chocolate, a half-hour break, and a lesson on how to disarm a gunman coming up."

CHAPTER 24

Cole headed for the service door designated for those carrying backstage access passes, Isabelle and Marit flanked between him and Lars. He wasn't thrilled that Isabelle would no longer be able to carry his spare weapon with her due to the higher security measures present at the Louvre. His determination to stick close to both her and Marit was rising by the minute.

Lars slowed as they approached the entrance and the guard standing beside it. Despite the meter of space and two women between them, Cole didn't miss the way Lars gripped the forged pass hanging from his neck.

Lars put his arm around Marit and leaned toward Cole, his voice low. "Are you sure this is going to work?"

"Trust me." Cole slid his arm around Isabelle, both to draw closer to Lars and to take advantage of her nearness. "Act like you're supposed to be here."

"I am supposed to be here," Lars said. "Just not like this."

"Keep that to yourself," Cole whispered.

"Everything will be fine," Isabelle assured Lars. She cast a glance at Marit. "At least with getting inside."

"You're going to be great today," Marit said. "Just remember, one step at a time."

"Right."

They reached the entrance, and Cole held up his backstage pass. He had to admit, whoever at the CIA had created it was seriously talented. After picking it up from the Paris station, he had compared the forged passes to Isabelle's. Even when placed side by side, Cole couldn't tell which one was real and which was fake.

The guard leaned closer to inspect Cole's pass. Then he waved him through. Lars followed without incident.

Cole waited for Lars to catch up to him. "See? I told you not to worry."

"In my defense, you've told me that a lot of times, including when people have been pointing guns at us."

Cole paused and thought back to the few times when he and Lars had ended up in dicey situations together. "I'm pretty sure you're exaggerating. I don't think I've said that when anyone was shooting."

"The fact that you had to think about it is proof enough for me."

"He may have a point." Marit took the lead, guiding them past signs that would soon direct ticket holders to where they needed to go.

Above him, light filtered through the pyramid-shaped windows in the ceiling, competing with the harsh lamps set up along the path that would be used as the runway. Beyond it, partitions and heavy black curtains created the backstage area.

Another guard stood by an opening in the curtain of the cordoned-off area reserved for the models, designers, and support staff for the upcoming show.

Now Isabelle's steps slowed.

"Are you okay?" Cole asked.

She shook her head. "You realize how insane this is, right?" She leaned closer and whispered, "I'm not a real model, no matter how much I'm pretending to be one."

"No, but you're doing a great job of making everyone believe you are." Cole pressed a kiss to her cheek. "I'm sure you'll be fantastic."

"Just pray that I don't trip."

"I can do that."

Marit walked past the guard and through the gap in the curtains. After flashing his pass again, Cole followed with Isabelle by his side.

He wasn't sure what he expected, but the scene in front of him wasn't it. Two long rows of styling stations ran down the center of the open space, the mirrors facing each other. It was as if a hair salon and a high-end makeup counter had joined forces and multiplied.

Racks of clothing lined the far wall, a few privacy screens interspersed among them.

Pieces of tape marked the floor like a ladder missing its side posts.

What appeared to be marble pillars framed the far side of the room where white curtains hung beside myriad portable lights. A couple of rolling cabinets had been pushed to the side of the nearest partition, both of them closed.

Camille Allard approached, relief on her face. "Isabelle, come with me. We changed the walk order."

Panic flashed in Isabelle's eyes.

Marit put a comforting hand on Isabelle's shoulder. "I'll see you in makeup."

Cole gave Isabelle's arm an encouraging squeeze. "Good luck today."

"Thanks."

Marit took several steps forward. "I'll see you later."

Cole fought the urge to remind Marit where to plant the hidden cameras. Marit and Isabelle knew what they were doing. They had already gone over their plans. He needed to trust her to execute her part of it.

"Where do we start?" Lars asked.

Cole reached out and pulled on the handle of the nearest cabinet. Locked.

Lars offered him a curious look. "What are you checking that for?"

"Just wondering what's inside." Cole scanned the area. Several models had arrived before them. He recognized Nadia talking to someone beside a rack of clothing. A couple dozen stylists and makeup artists already manned the mirrored stations in the center.

Suspecting they wouldn't have much time before they would be in the way of the show's preparations, Cole said, "I'll work my way around that side of the area. You check out this side."

"What am I looking for?"

"Anyone who doesn't belong."

"Besides us?" Lars asked.

"Yes. Besides us." Cole pointed at Lars's camera bag. "And take photos. Lots of photos."

"Now you're talking."

Isabelle was still recovering from Camille Allard's announcement that she had moved Isabelle to third on the runway when she found Marit sitting in front of a mirror, a hair stylist teasing her blonde hair into a windswept look.

Marguerite, the makeup artist assigned to help Isabelle for this show, circled behind her. "Sit. Sit. We have work to do." Marguerite pressed her hands against Isabelle's shoulders and guided her to the chair beside Marit.

"What did Camille change in the order?" Marit asked.

"She swapped me and Nadia."

Marit's eyes widened. "In the opening series?"

"Yeah." Isabelle swallowed hard. "How did I get myself into this again? I'm a banker, for heaven's sake." *And a spy*, Isabelle thought.

"You're a good friend. You've already saved my life more than once because you've been willing to do this." Marit reached out and put her hand on Isabelle's arm. "Thank you for being here." The sincerity in Marit's voice eased Isabelle's nerves slightly.

"Close your eyes," Marguerite instructed.

Isabelle obeyed. Within seconds, Marguerite had applied eye shadow to Isabelle's eyelids.

"Just so you know," Marit said. "There is one good thing about going early in the lineup."

"What's that?"

"You'll get to take your shoes off sooner than the rest of us."

"Only to have to put on a new pair a few minutes later."

"Yes, but the first pair you're wearing is an inch higher than the second."

"True." *Concentrate on the positives.* Isabelle repeated that thought over and over again. For the next twenty-five minutes, Isabelle continued to follow her stylist's instructions: Look up. Look down. Purse your lips. Turn this way. Now the other way.

Her hair came next. First, the stylist used a curling iron to create ringlets in Isabelle's long, auburn hair, followed by more hair spray than should ever be released in an indoor setting. The stylists then pinned white forget-me-nots into her curls, the white petals contrasting against the darkness of her hair.

"One hour!" one of Camille's assistants shouted from the front of the backstage area.

The next forty-five minutes passed by in a blur, all the models getting dressed, Camille inspecting each of her designs. She reached Isabelle, and Isabelle lifted her chin slightly, the way Marit had taught her.

Camille stared at her creation, Isabelle little more than the hanger displaying it. After several seconds, she tugged at the edge of Isabelle's sleeve. "Good. Very good."

"Ten minutes!" came the next warning.

This was really happening. Isabelle was standing backstage at Fashion Week, in the Carrousel du Louvre, no less, wearing a beautiful gown that would take two paychecks of her bank executive's salary to buy, and she was going third down the runway of her first fashion show ever.

She tried to wiggle her toes, unable to do so in the four-inch heels currently squeezing her feet. Maybe Marit was right about going early so she could take these off. She could already feel the blisters forming on her little toes.

"Five minutes!"

Isabelle's stomach lurched uncomfortably.

Her assistant, Ellie, adjusted the sleeve of her dress again. "Breathe."

"Right." Isabelle drew in a deep breath. In her head, she repeated Marit's many instructions. Chin up, eyes forward, one foot in front of the other, attitude, a little smile.

Lights flickered for several seconds, signaling the beginning of the show. Then the music started.

Isabelle's chest tightened, her whole body trembled, and then suddenly, the two women in front of her were walking the floor, and it was her turn.

One foot in front of the other, she repeated in her mind. She stepped past the white gauzy curtains and got her first look at the audience. Chairs lined either side of what was basically a wide hallway, with more chairs at the end of the space designated as the runway.

Isabelle strode forward, her chin up until she reached the spot where she was supposed to pause. She struck a pose the way Marit had taught her, pivoted once to allow the audience to see her from the other side, and then again to turn back. Placing each step deliberately, she continued up the runway to where she had started. The moment she passed by the curtains, a sigh of relief escaped her.

Marit, who was currently five spots back, grinned at her. "Congrats. You're now a runway model."

Isabelle simply shook her head. "No," she whispered. "But thank you for making it possible for me to pretend."

Ellie rushed forward and tugged at Isabelle's arm. "Hurry up. You need to change."

Isabelle simply nodded. "I'm coming."

As far as Marit was concerned, Paris was at its finest at night. The full moon shining down on the Seine, the lights, the romantic music spilling out from the cafés and restaurants, and the people strolling along the pavement, soaking up the ambiance of the city. If it weren't for the fact that muggers and pickpockets also thrived in this environment, it would be practically perfect.

She shifted a little closer to Lars, and the arm he'd placed around her waist tightened. Tonight would be different. After Camille Allard's show had ended, they'd stopped at the flat long enough for her and Isabelle to drop off their purses and change into comfortable shoes and had then gone to the restaurant Cole had booked for them. Without her purse, she was no longer a target. At least, she hoped not.

Cole and Isabelle were walking hand in hand a couple of meters ahead of her and Lars. They stopped at the corner of the street, waiting to cross.

"I think we should celebrate Isabelle's success like this after every show," Lars said as they came up behind them.

Cole looked over his shoulder and grinned. "The bœuf bourguignon, the profiteroles, or the walk along the Seine?"

"All of it," Lars said.

"How about we do all those things without me having to work any more shows?" Isabelle suggested hopefully.

Marit shook her head. "I hate to break it to you and your tired feet, Isabelle, but you're a natural. I'm not kidding. Very few women could pull off what you did today, and you did it with only a few minutes' instruction."

"You both did a great job placing the hidden cameras backstage too." Cole took his phone out of his pocket and pulled up a couple of images. Now that the show was over and the overhead lights were off, the area where the models left their personal belongings was in shadow. The security lights were just strong enough to outline the empty white cubbies and a meter or so of the floor around them.

"Even though no one went after the purse today, it's probably a good thing we set the cameras up when we did," Marit said. "Tomorrow's going to be a whole lot crazier backstage. Valentino's show will bring in a lot of big names and a huge number of models. They'll barely have time to clear out Valentino's crew before Li Du and his people need to set up."

The traffic signals changed, and they crossed the road together. Weaving around the trees lining the pavement, they continued walking toward the closest bridge.

"I'm glad we're not working Valentino's show," Isabelle said. "Apart from the stress, I'm not sure that my feet would survive two shows back-to-back like that."

"They're going to have to," Marit said. "The day after tomorrow, we have Peter Wade in the morning and Kyle Adams in the evening."

Isabelle groaned. "I knew that. How could I have forgotten?"

"For a model at Fashion Week, taking one day at a time is a matter of self-preservation," Marit said.

"Is Henri LaRue's show in the morning or evening?" Lars asked.

"His show's in the evening, three days after Wade's and Adams's," Marit said. "And two days after that is Molenaar."

"LaRue caught a lucky break, being placed ahead of Molenaar in the lineup," Cole said.

"He did," Marit said. "Even though most designers hope for the last spots so that their designs are the ones fresh on people's minds when everyone leaves."

"They each aspire to end Fashion Week with a bang," Lars said.

Cole grimaced. "Pretty sure there's going to be a bang this time round. I just don't know how big it will be."

CHAPTER 25

Cole stood near the curtain where the models would come out once the next show began. Beside him, Lars held up his camera as the crowd from the Valentino show dispersed, his current focus an older woman wearing a ridiculous feathered hat.

Cole had to give his cousin credit. He had a way of capturing an image, and he was doing a great job of making sure they were able to document everyone present at the various shows that Marit and Isabelle were modeling in.

"Any sign of LaRue?" Cole asked, his voice low.

"Not yet." Lars lowered his camera briefly and nodded at the cell phone in Cole's hand. "Any luck backstage?"

"No." Cole returned his attention to the surveillance images on his screen. Marit and Isabelle really had done a great job of planting the two cameras. They angled across the front of the wooden cubbies to show everyone accessing them, but the angle protected the privacy of the dressing area beyond them.

On another app, the current location of the purse illuminated his screen. The small tracking device was a simple one he had tucked inside the inner pocket, but it would show them if the purse went into motion when it wasn't supposed to.

Two models appeared on the top part of his screen, both of them with purses hanging from their shoulders. They each slid their bags into a cubby and disappeared back the way they had come.

Marit and Isabelle arrived next. Lars must have been watching for them, because he leaned closer so he could see Cole's screen better.

"I'm not sure who is more nervous about leaving her purse, Marit or Isabelle," Lars said.

"After seeing the price tag associated with the bag we borrowed for Isabelle, it's probably her, although since Marit's bag is also a Ralph Molenaar original, I'd prefer not to have to replace either one."

"After having two people try to steal Marit's bag, Marit is probably relieved to not have it hanging off her shoulder."

"True." Cole glanced up at the now-empty rows of chairs. Two staff members straightened them while two more swept the runway.

A security guard approached Cole and Lars and spoke in French.

"What did he say?" Cole asked Lars.

"He said everyone needs to clear out between shows."

Cole held up his all-access pass. "Lars, show him yours."

Lars followed Cole's instructions. After a closer inspection, the guard nodded and moved on.

"It's official. I like these passes better than the media one Coster gave me," Lars said.

"Me too." Cole returned his attention to his cell phone screen, where Marit's and Isabelle's bags were clearly visible on camera two.

Several minutes passed with the museum clean-up crew finishing their task and the models in the backstage area checking in and stowing their belongings.

More than a half hour passed before Lars lifted his camera, signaling the arrival of the patrons for Li Du's show.

A model came into view on camera one, continuing into the image until she was visible on both screens. She stopped in front of the cubbies, temporarily blocking Cole's view of Marit's bag.

When the woman with the bright-yellow blouse and long dark hair stepped out of the way, Marit's bag was no longer in place.

"Lars." Cole held out his phone for his cousin to see. "Someone just took Marit's bag."

"Let's go." Lars started toward the backstage area, but Cole grabbed his arm.

"I'll go. You keep an eye out here," Cole said. "Watch for a model with a yellow blouse and long dark hair."

"Carrying Marit's bag."

"Yes." Taking the most direct route to the cubbies, Cole flashed his badge at the guard beside the runway entrance and slipped past the curtain into the backstage area. He recognized his mistake too late. People everywhere. Models walking to and from the makeup area. Others standing by the dressing area. Li Du and several of his design team were scattered beside the tape affixed to the floor a short distance away, the first models already standing in their designated spots.

Someone rushed by holding a gown as long as two wedding dresses combined.

Cole stepped to the side, searching for the woman in yellow. Bright colors appeared to be the name of the game in Li Du's line: purple, blue, red . . . and yellow. Cole spotted a flash of the color he was looking for and stepped closer to where the bags were stored. He made it two steps before he caught a full view of the model wearing the sunshine-colored dress, her blonde hair flowing loosely over her back.

Cole worked his way forward, scanning the area once more. He was all the way to the makeup area before he spotted the woman who had taken Marit's purse. Or was it? Surely someone who had just committed a crime wouldn't be sitting in a stylist's chair as though she didn't have a care in the world other than puckering her lips while the makeup artist applied lipstick.

Cole retrieved the security feed he had captured on his phone, rewound it, and pulled up the woman's image. No doubt about it. He'd found the thief.

Cole stepped past three stylists and stopped behind the woman in the yellow blouse. The stylist capped the lipstick and looked up at him. "You can't be in this area."

"I'll leave as soon as she returns the bag she stole."

The model looked up at the reflection of Cole in the mirror in front of them. "I didn't steal anything."

"I saw you take Marit Jansen's bag from the cubby a minute ago."

"Are you talking about the oversized white Molenaar purse?"

Cole wouldn't have known about the brand had Marit and Isabelle not already pointed it out to him. "That's the one."

"That wasn't Marit's. It belonged to one of the models from the Valentino show."

"Who told you that?" Cole asked.

"Felicia."

"Where is she?"

This time the stylist answered. "Over there. Eight chairs down on the right. She's wearing a pink apron."

"Thanks." Cole headed the way the stylist pointed. He counted off the chairs and found the woman with crinkly brown hair and a pink apron. "Are you Felicia?"

"*Oui.*" She turned, a curling iron gripped in her hand.

"Where's the purse?" Cole asked. "The white one the model gave you."

Felicia jutted her chin toward the main backstage entrance. "A guard asked for it. He said one of the Valentino models left it but that she wasn't allowed backstage after the show ended."

Cole spotted the guard by the curtain. "Was it him?"

"No. The man I spoke to was shorter. And his hair was blond, not brown."

"Thanks." Cole pulled up the app on his phone to determine the location of the purse. The blue circle that identified the tracking device flashed, moving slightly one way and then the other. Not able to determine the exact location, Cole backtracked past the stylist chairs and made his way to the guard by the curtain. "Do you know where the other guard went? The blond one? He's a bit shorter than you?"

"He left a minute ago," he said in a thick French accent. "He was returning a lost item."

"What's his name?"

"I don't know. I'd never met him before."

Cole pulled out his phone and called Lars. "Lars, keep an eye out for a blond security guard, under six feet tall, carrying Marit's bag."

"He got past you?" Lars asked incredulously.

Cole looked down at the app on his phone, the blue dot simply indicating that the purse was somewhere in the Louvre. "Yeah." He let out a frustrated sigh. "He got past me."

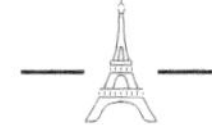

Lars scanned the crowded room. Those who'd come to Valentino's show had already exited, but the incoming crowd was causing congestion at the doors. Although many people had claimed seats, more of them had not. The aisles were full of people, and far too many of them were blond-haired men around six feet tall.

Barely resisting the temptation to stand on the nearest chair so that he could see over the heads of those milling around the room, Lars hurried to the nearest aisle and started for the door. If the thief had already escaped the backstage area, the first thing he'd do was make for the exit.

Navigating around several tripods and camera cases, Lars made it only two meters before a large woman wearing an enormous, floppy hat blocked his path.

"*Excusez-moi.*" He shifted half a pace to the left. She didn't move. He tried going right. She still didn't move.

Gritting his teeth, he stepped onto the empty chair beside him, straddled the back, and lowered himself into the next row. The rim of the floppy hat rippled as the woman turned her head to give him a look of consternation. Lars ignored her. Darting back into the aisle, he wove past the next three people, all the while scouring the area for anyone in a security-guard uniform.

Someone shouted. Lars looked left. A man in a black suit was signaling to a woman wearing a bright-red creation. Lars couldn't tell exactly what it was. It was one-third dress, one-third trousers, one-third tent. But it made an impression. People parted as she moved, and in the gap she left in her wake, he spotted a blond-haired security guard.

A quick look up the congested aisle told him he'd never reach the door before the security guard was out of the room. Making a snap decision, he moved into the nearest row, worked his way down until he reached a cluster of empty chairs, and then started climbing over them.

"Hey! What d'you think you're doing?" It was a man's voice, but Lars didn't bother turning around to identify him.

"Security!"

This time, the shout came from a woman. Lars didn't mind at all. A little help from security right now would be welcome. Unless it came from the guy he was trying to catch.

Lars clamored over two more rows before dropping to the floor and hurrying back to the aisle. Those who were seated nearby gave him disapproving looks, but it appeared that the security guards were having as much difficulty reaching him as he was having in trying to get out. There wasn't a guard anywhere near him.

"Sorry," he panted. "It's an emergency."

Some of the disapproving looks turned disbelieving. Lars kept moving. He darted around two women dressed like flower gardens and caught another glimpse of the security guard one second before the man disappeared through the open door.

Pushing past the group of people standing at the entrance, Lars burst into the outer foyer. It was as crowded as the area behind him. And the only people wearing a security-guard uniform in sight were the tall, dark-haired man and short, balding man checking for tickets at the door.

"Any sign of him?" At the sound of Cole's breathless voice, Lars swung around.

"I thought I spotted him, but I couldn't get out here fast enough."

Cole's frustrated expression matched Lars's feelings perfectly. "Whoever it was had help." He pulled out his phone.

"Who are you calling?" Lars asked.

"I was going to text the girls to tell them."

"Don't bother," Lars said. "They won't be able to access their phones until the show's over."

Isabelle had survived another show. Two down, four to go. She hoped her feet would survive that long. Leaning down, she eased her foot out of the three-inch heel, wincing when the back rubbed against a particularly raw blister.

A sigh of relief escaped her the moment both shoes were back on the rack. She changed out of the oversized black dress and into her own clothes. When she opened the curtain of her dressing stall, Marit waited outside.

"You did really well today." Marit gave her a hug.

"Thanks. I feel like we need to celebrate every time we finish a show."

"Most people feel that way. That's why there are so many parties during Fashion Week."

"Personally, I prefer the quiet celebrations with our boyfriends over the ones with cameras flashing everywhere."

Marit leaned close and whispered. "You and me both." She looked at Isabelle's bare feet. "Are you about ready?"

"Yes." Rather than put her shoes on, she hooked them on the fingers of her right hand—no way was she putting them on before absolutely necessary—and headed for the cubbies, where she had left her borrowed bag.

Cole and Lars waited beside them, their faces grim.

A crease formed on Marit's brow. "This doesn't look good."

"No, it doesn't." She and Marit reached the men. "I feel like I'm asking this question a lot, but is everything okay?"

Cole shook his head. "We lost Marit's bag."

Marit's shoulders slumped, and disappointment colored her expression. "What about the tracking device?"

"Someone must have found it, because it went offline not long after the purse was stolen," Cole said.

Lars slid his arm around Marit's shoulders. "We're really sorry, Marit."

"Did you see who took it?" Marit asked.

"Yes, but it wasn't the person who ended up with it," Cole said. He explained the progression of events.

"Did you ever identify the guard?" Isabelle asked.

"No. He came in with fake credentials, but the security cameras caught a decent image of him, so police are running his image through facial ID."

The police would hopefully find out who the culprit was, but if the Paris police department was anything like the ones in the large cities in the States, it could take days to get results.

Isabelle's gaze met Cole's. "Maybe you should have your friends run the image too."

"I already forwarded it over." Cole retrieved Isabelle's borrowed Molenaar bag and handed it to her. "My guess is he's another hired hand."

"Whoever's behind this is spending a lot of money trying to get these designs," Marit said. "That's at least three people they've sent after my purse."

"Maybe we need to start looking for large withdrawals from LaRue's bank accounts," Isabelle said. "That could help tie him to the attempted muggings."

Lars put his hand on Marit's waist as they all started toward the exit. "I don't suppose he's one of the designers who banks with Bankhaus Steiner, is he?"

"I'm afraid not, but I know some people who might be able to check out his transactions," Isabelle said.

"Between Cole's friends and your friends, you two really do make a great team," Lars said.

Cole took her hand and brought it to his lips. "Yes, we do."

Goose bumps formed along her arm and up her neck at the simple gesture. Cole really could be charming at times. And completely clueless at others. Perhaps it was the unpredictability that kept her on her toes and left her always enjoying the question of what he would do next.

She stopped when they reached the main hallway to slip her shoes on and winced when one rubbed against her heel.

"You okay?" Cole asked.

"I will be as soon as I put on some fresh Band-Aids, or plasters, or whatever you want to call them."

"Do we need to pick up some more at the pharmacy?" Cole asked.

"I have plenty in my—" Marit broke off. "Purse . . . or I did."

"Looks like we need to make a stop on the way back to the flat," Cole said.

They reached the exit, Isabelle only limping slightly as she went.

As soon as they were outside, Lars said, "What's our plan for tonight? Find someplace to eat and commiserate over Marit's lost bag, or stop at the pharmacy first so Isabelle can find some relief?"

"Pharmacy first," Isabelle insisted. "After that, anywhere you want to go is fine."

"There's a pharmacy right down the street," Marit said.

Cole and Isabelle fell into step behind Lars and Marit. The way he deliberately kept Marit and Lars in front of them suggested that Cole either had something to say that he didn't want them to hear, or he wanted to make sure he could block any threat that might approach them from behind.

Cole leaned close. "How long will it take you to pull the financials on LaRue?"

"If I send the request to headquarters, I could have them as early as tomorrow," Isabelle said. "I think we need to request that finance runs the same search on our other suspects, too, just to be safe."

"As long as I don't have to stare at spreadsheets, you can request as many reports as you want."

"I had a feeling you would say that," Isabelle said.

They reached the pharmacy, where Lars and Marit were still standing outside.

"Lars and I will wait here," Cole said.

Marit stepped inside. "I'll help you find them."

"Thanks," Isabelle said as they headed toward the correct aisle. Isabelle took a box off the shelf. She looked down at her feet and then at Marit. "I should probably get two boxes, shouldn't I?'

"I'm afraid so."

CHAPTER 26

Cole secured his laptop in his bag and slipped the strap over his shoulder. He and Isabelle had yet to receive any updates on the identity of the thief from yesterday's show or the financial records Isabelle had requested from CIA headquarters.

Isabelle, Marit, and Lars waited by the door.

"Are you ready?" Isabelle asked him.

"I think the more important question is, Are *you* ready?" Cole asked.

"I've already bandaged my blisters, so I'm probably as ready as I'm going to get."

Cole's phone rang. He pulled it out, intending to silence it, but when he saw Jasmine's name on his screen, he hit the Talk button. "Anything new?"

"Yes. The fake security guard popped up in Interpol's database."

"Who is he?" Cole asked.

"Jemond Mercier. He was arrested six years ago in Paris for forgery."

"That would explain how he came up with fake credentials to get into the Louvre." Cole glanced at the others, who were still waiting for him at the door. "We're heading out now to the next fashion show, but let me know if you find anything else."

"There's more," Jasmine said. "I just emailed you and Isabelle the financials for the top six designers on your suspect list. If you need me to have headquarters pull any more, let me know."

"Thanks, Jazz. I will." Cole ended the call.

"What did she say?" Isabelle asked.

"She found the ID of our purse thief. He's a forger who was arrested in Paris a few years ago," Cole said. "She also emailed me some new information."

"Are you ready?" Marit asked. "We really need to get going."

Cole didn't like the idea of sending them on alone. Even though Marit's purse had been stolen, whoever was behind the theft hadn't gotten what he wanted. If the thief still believed Marit had the flash drive, she was in just as much danger now as before they had set their trap.

"Do you want me to escort Marit and Isabelle to the show while you look at your new information?" Lars asked.

Cole debated briefly. Then he caught the expression on Isabelle's face, the one that indicated that she was perfectly capable of taking care of herself, blisters or not.

"Maybe I will stay and check out the new intel," Cole said. "I'll catch up with you as soon as I can."

"Sounds good." Lars opened the door.

"Hey, Lars?" Cole called after him. "Since I won't be there, make sure you set up near the front of the runway, where you can see the whole crowd."

"What about the backstage area?" Lars asked.

"Isabelle will be with Marit," Cole said. "And the police have people standing by."

"True." Lars nodded and escorted Marit into the hall.

Isabelle lingered and gave him a quick kiss. She kept her face close to his and whispered, "I'll keep my phone with me as long as I can. Let me know if you need any help deciphering the financials."

"I can't believe I have to analyze spreadsheets."

"You aren't analyzing spreadsheets. You're analyzing bank and credit card statements."

Cole grimaced. "That's not any better."

"Good luck." Isabelle gave him one more kiss and headed for the door.

"You too."

"Thanks." She closed the door behind her, and Cole pulled his laptop from his bag.

"Time to get this over with," he muttered to himself, settling down at the kitchen table and pulling up the files Jasmine had sent.

He keyed in on the banking and credit card information from Henri LaRue and pulled up the file. He scanned over the various line items, searching for any large cash withdrawals or credit card advances. When he didn't find any, he looked over the numbers again, this time trying to identify what the various expenses represented.

The payroll appeared to run through one bank account, the numbers fluctuating at various times of the year. It didn't take long to figure out that the spikes in payroll occurred in the weeks right before the various Fashion Week events and extended to the two weeks after they concluded.

After going over the payroll account twice without finding anything that connected LaRue to James, Cole pulled up LaRue's main operating account as well as his credit cards. Again, the expenses were clustered, but this time, the high points occurred in the two months before Fashion Week. From what he could tell, a large portion of the expenses were for fabric and supplies as well as airline tickets. Hotel charges were the outlier, not occurring until the end of Fashion Week.

Cole went over the expenses a second time, but nothing flagged as a possible cash payout or anything else that would be outside the norm for someone in the design business.

Disappointed that nothing was pointing a finger at LaRue, he glanced at the clock. He'd been staring at financial information for more than an hour. Isabelle would undoubtedly be able to perform this task in a fraction of the time.

With a sigh, he moved to the next set of financials, these for Peter Wade. Maybe if he compared the timing of expenses, he would be able to see if a payment was out of place and was actually being funneled through a third party.

As he had with LaRue's accounts, Cole started with payroll. Peter Wade's expenses ran a bit higher than LaRue's but not by much. When he moved to the expense and credit card accounts, the numbers also fell into a similar category, except that Peter Wade's deposits were significantly higher than LaRue's, as was his current bank account balance.

Moving on, Cole opened Li Du's account. He did a quick skim of his budget in case there were any large cash deposits. Again, nothing. Then again, Li Du's show had already occurred. Surely, if he had been behind the theft of Ralph's designs, they would have seen some sign of it yesterday.

With that thought in mind, Cole focused on the only other designer who hadn't yet shown his line but who had also started on their suspect list: Kyle Adams.

A text buzzed on his phone, and Cole pulled it up. Isabelle walking down the runway in a red pantsuit, her chin up, a little smile on her face. The Peter Wade show was underway, and he was missing it.

Determined to finish this analysis before the Kyle Adams show tonight, he hit the thumbs-up button on the photo Lars had sent him and turned his attention back to his laptop screen.

The payroll accounts looked much like the other three he had already researched. He pulled up Adams's credit cards, the first two showing normal activity. When he reached the third, he skimmed over the pending charges, which included a four-hundred-euro expense yesterday at a hotel along with a large restaurant bill last night. He continued down the list, several of the next charges catching his attention. An Air France bill for over six thousand dollars preceded by a KLM charge for twelve hundred dollars.

Cole checked the dates. The airline ticket purchased on KLM occurred the day after the robbery at Ralph's office. The other tickets were purchased three days later.

Cole grabbed his phone and dialed Jasmine. As soon as she answered, he said, "Hey, I need you to access some airline data for me."

"What do you need?" Jasmine asked.

"Passenger names and flight dates. The first is for KLM. All I have is the credit card info."

"If it's off the financials I sent you, tell me where to look."

Cole relayed the credit card account information.

"Got it." Jasmine fell silent. "I assume you want the details on the Air France flights too."

"Yes."

"This may take a minute."

Cole checked the time on his computer. Peter Wade's show was long over, and Kyle Adams's show would begin in less than a half hour. "We don't have a lot of time on this."

"Hold on," Jasmine said as though calming an impatient child.

Cole gritted his teeth. He needed to get over to the Louvre, and he wanted Isabelle and Marit in his sight.

The clicking of a keyboard carried over the line. "Also, I was about to call you. I found an interesting tidbit today."

"What's that?"

"Did you know that James used to intern for Kyle Adams?"

"What?"

"Could be that Adams used James to gain access to Molenaar's designs."

"That would make sense."

"Okay, I've got the first one. Corbin Butler," Jasmine said.

"I'll pull his info if you'll look up the Air France passengers."

"You got it." Jasmine relayed the man's US passport info.

Cole tapped into the State Department's database and did a search for Corbin Butler. It took only a minute to retrieve his personal information and five more minutes to retrieve the name of his current employer: Kyle Adams.

"I think we found the designer behind Ralph Molenaar's design theft," Cole said. "The man on the KLM flight is one of his employees, and he left the day after James was killed—probably with Molenaar's muslin patterns. My guess is Kyle went to pick up the designs from James, and either James got greedy, or Adams lost it when he found out James had dropped the flash drive into Marit's purse."

"It's possible, but the fact that his employee flew to the States the next day isn't concrete evidence he was involved," Jasmine said.

"But it is suspicious."

"Yes, it is."

"If we can find evidence of Adams using Molenaar's designs, the police will at least be able to tie him to the theft."

"True." Jasmine paused. "Okay, I have the other passengers; all four are women in their early twenties."

"Why would Adams pay so much money to buy last-minute tickets for four women?" Cole asked. "Unless . . ."

"Unless they're his models for the new clothes he had made from Molenaar's designs," Jasmine finished for him. "I'm looking at their passport photos. All four women are beautiful."

"I need to get over to the show. It's starting in a few minutes."

"Do you want me to call the police for you?"

"That would be great. Call Capitaine Dupont. His phone number should be in my report."

"I have it," Jasmine said. "Be careful."

"I will," Cole said. "As long as Adams doesn't know we're on to him, he isn't a threat."

"He may have killed Brinton James," Jasmine reminded him. "Don't underestimate what the man is capable of."

"I won't." Cole hung up and secured his laptop. As soon as it was locked away, he rushed out the door. He debated briefly calling Lars, but Jasmine's last comment carried with him. Adams could very well be capable of murder. Cole couldn't take a chance that Lars, Isabelle, or Marit might inadvertently alert Adams that he was suspected of both theft and murder.

With expediency in mind, Cole rushed to the elevator and used his phone to summon a taxi.

CHAPTER 27

The stylist reached for an enormous can of hair spray. Marit closed her eyes, holding her breath as the strong-smelling cloud enveloped her head. The stylist tweaked one piece of hair and then stepped back from the chair.

"Okay," she said. "You're good to go."

"Thanks." Marit rose to make room for the next model. It was Isabelle. "You look amazing," Marit whispered as they traded places.

The makeup artist had worked a new kind of magic this time; Isabelle's stunning green eyes were impossible to ignore. Marit smiled as she headed to the clothing racks. She almost felt sorry for Cole. No matter his tough-guy exterior, one look at Isabelle today and he'd be sunk.

Brookelyn, her assistant for this show, was standing near the clothing racks, waiting for her with a bright-purple garment draped across her arm. "I'm glad Felicia took a little longer than usual on your hair," she said. "Someone added more clothes to the rack, and the jumpsuit wasn't where it was supposed to be. It took me a minute to find it."

Marit glanced at the rack. It did look fuller than it had during rehearsals. "Did they lose a rack and have to consolidate?"

"I don't think so," Brookelyn said. "Hannah saw me trying to find the jumpsuit and came over to help. She said at least a dozen more pieces have been added to Mr. Adams's show since rehearsals."

Over a dozen new outfits. That wasn't supposed to happen. The whole reason for a dress rehearsal was to give everyone backstage the chance to make sure they knew exactly when each model and outfit hit the runway. Adding only one would mess up the order of events. Adding a dozen could be disastrous.

"Have they changed the runway order?" Marit asked.

"Yes." Anxiety shone in Brookelyn's eyes. "You have a little more time between the first and second change, but a little less between the second and third."

"Who's modeling the new stuff?"

Brookelyn shrugged. "I think they called in some extra girls." She glanced over her shoulder. "There are a few here who I didn't see at rehearsals."

Marit had been one of the first models to arrive and had been taken into hair and makeup immediately. Now she took a moment to look around. The number of people backstage had increased considerably, and she instantly spotted four models who hadn't been at the rehearsal. In fact, as far as she knew, they hadn't even been at the castings.

"If they only just got here, how did they do the fittings?" Marit asked, hurrying to the curtained-off area so she could change into the jumpsuit.

"I don't know." Brookelyn slipped in with her, holding the outfit so that Marit could step into it as soon as she'd taken off her jeans. "Maybe they did it before they arrived. They're all Americans."

Marit froze, one leg in the jumpsuit, the other in her jeans. "What did you say?"

"The new models. They're . . . they're all American." Brookelyn gave her a worried look. "Is there something wrong with that?"

"No." Marit tossed her jeans aside, her thoughts whirling. Cole and Lars had taken Adams off the suspect list when they'd learned that he had no local facility to produce clothing. But what if he'd sent the muslin patterns to the States, produced the clothing, and then had them fitted to American models there?

Brookelyn stepped around Marit to pull up her zipper. The moment the garment was on, Marit stepped out of the changing area, but instead of taking her place in the lineup, she veered back to the clothing rack.

"Show me where the new clothes are, Brookelyn," she said.

Brookelyn's look of concern had yet to disappear. "I didn't mean to complain. I can manage."

"I'm sure you can. And you'll do much more than manage." Marit worked to keep her impatience in check. "I'm just curious to see what's been added."

Brookelyn led her to the far end of the rack. "Some of them are mixed in with the others," she said, "but most of them are at the end." She pulled out a blue gown.

Marit's mouth went dry. The dress was identical to the blue gown she'd worn during Ralph's dress rehearsal. Stepping closer, she reached for the gown beside it. The shimmery gold fabric sparkled under the overhead lights—just as it had when Nadia had worn it. But Nadia wasn't working Kyle Adams's show.

One of the American models must be scheduled to wear this garment as part of his grand finale.

Indignation and a new sense of urgency coursed through her. "How much time do I have before I'm up?"

Brookelyn glanced at the curtain that led to the runway. The stage coordinator, with her clipboard in hand, was consulting with the model standing at the front of the line. Above her head, a large clock was counting down seconds. "Sixteen to seventeen minutes," she said. "There's another fifteen and a half minutes before the show starts, and you're third in line." She eyed the jumpsuit Marit was wearing, obviously looking for something out of place. "Do you need something?"

"Yes," Marit said grimly. "Answers." She glanced over her shoulder. Isabelle was still in the stylist's chair. It would be impossible to have a private conversation with her until she was out of it. On the original schedule, Isabelle was the tenth model to walk. It was probable that one or more of the Americans had been inserted ahead of her, and if that were the case, Marit would have to act quickly if she was to prevent one of Ralph's designs from appearing on the runway in Adams's show. There was no time to check the schedule. The time remaining to her had dropped below fifteen minutes already.

"I have to make a phone call," she said.

"But you're due—"

Marit didn't wait to hear the rest. She ran for the cubbies, where Isabelle had left her purse. Grateful that she'd placed her phone in Isabelle's bag for safekeeping before her own purse had been stolen, she grabbed the bag Ralph had loaned Isabelle and started rooting through it. Keys, tissues, pens, lip gloss. Finally, her fingers found a phone. She pulled it out, dismayed to discover that it was Isabelle's. Lars's and Cole's number were definitely on this phone, but Marit didn't know Isabelle's passcode. Setting the phone aside, she dug out a notebook and a brush before finally locating her own phone at the very bottom of the bag.

Her heart racing, she touched the screen. She was down to thirteen minutes before the show began. With all the noise outside, Lars may not hear the phone, and she didn't have time to make a second call. Pulling up Cole's number, she pushed Call and put the phone to her ear. She glanced around the room. Where could she go that wasn't so far away that she'd never make it to the curtain in time but that gave her a modicum of privacy in this chaotic space?

The corner. One wall was a curtain, but she could turn her back to the crowd.

After the second ring, Cole's voice came on. "Are you okay?"

"Yes." She lowered her voice. "It's Kyle Adams. Ralph's designs are hanging on the racks, and Adams brought in American models. He plans to pass the clothes off as his tonight."

"I'm on my way over there."

"Hurry. I don't know when the first one hits the runway."

"You know I will. And, Marit, I need you and Isabelle to act like you don't know anything. It's the only way to keep you safe until the authorities get there."

"I have to go. Will you call them?"

"Already on it." He disconnected the call.

"I don't allow my models to use their phones during a show, Miss Jansen."

Marit spun around. Adams stood in front of her, his dark eyes flashing.

"I'm sorry. I didn't know that," she managed. "It was an emergency."

He eyed her grimly. "So I gather."

Marit's stomach clenched. How much had he heard? *Pretend you don't know anything.* Cole's words echoed in her head.

"I'll put my phone away right now." When he made no move, she gestured toward the curtain. "I'm up in ten minutes, so I'd better get in line."

"Who were you talking to?"

"A friend."

His jaw clenched. "You were discussing my designs with someone else before they've debuted. I think that gives me the right to know his or her name."

The knot in Marit's stomach tightened. He'd heard everything.

"Marit Jansen." The woman at the head of the line called her name.

"If you'll excuse me, I'm needed at the front." With her heart pounding so hard she was sure he could hear it, Marit attempted to pass on Adams's left.

He reached out, grabbing her arm in a vicelike grip. "Give me your phone."

"I can leave it up front."

"The time for playing games is over, Miss Jansen." He moved to stand behind her, and she felt the barrel of a gun press between her shoulder blades. "Give me your phone."

All the self-defense lessons Isabelle and Cole had given her flashed before her eyes. If Adams had been standing in front of her, she might have had a chance of disarming him. But she had no idea how to overcome a gun at her back.

Her mind raced. If Adams was behind James's death, she couldn't risk calling out. He was already a murderer. There was no telling how many more he would injure or kill in this confined space full of people. Cole was on his way. He'd called the police. She just had to stay calm. Surely, someone would arrive in time to help her.

Slowly, she raised her phone. Keeping the gun firmly against her, he snatched it from her hand.

"Now we're going to go around the curtain," he said. "It might interest you to know that while it blocks you from view, it allows you to hear everything."

It was a not-so-subtle jab. Marit had been foolish. She'd also had very few options and even less time.

"Marit Jansen." It was the woman at the front of the line again.

"Someone will come looking for me," Marit said.

"Not when I tell them that you became suddenly and violently ill."

"What about the jumpsuit?" She was grasping at straws, but that was about all she had right now. "I'm still wearing it."

"I have more clothing items than I need for tonight's show," he said. "It won't be missed any more than you will be." They rounded the curtain. On the other side, there was a break in the temporary partitions. "That way." He pushed her toward the gap.

Marit walked through. The hall beyond was empty. No doubt, this part of the venue had been cordoned off. If there were any security guards in the vicinity, they were well hidden. Dragging her roughly across the hall, Adams pushed her face against a door.

"Take off the sash," he demanded.

With trembling fingers, Marit untied the bow around her waist and pulled the fabric free of the jumpsuit.

"Now open the door."

Grasping the knob, Marit turned it and pulled. The door swung open, releasing the overpowering smell of pine and lemon. It was a janitor's cupboard.

"Inside," he barked.

A door opened, releasing the rumble of distant voices. Adams gave her a push. Marit stumbled over a vacuum, but before she could fully regain her balance, he shoved her into the corner. Her impact against the wall was lessened by the presence of a mop head.

The potent aroma of pine-scented detergent burned her nose and made her eyes sting. She blinked several times before realizing that the gun was no longer at her back. She shifted.

"Don't move another inch." Adams was right behind her, and in one swift movement, he grabbed an extension cord from a hook on the wall. "Put your arms behind you."

Unwilling to comply, Marit swung her elbows back, attempting to connect with Adams's ribs. He must have sensed the movement because he grabbed her wrists, and almost before she knew what he was doing, he'd wrapped the extension cord around them.

She pivoted, swinging her leg upward. Her heel caught his knee. He swore, and his hand came down, hitting her across the face. Marit reeled back, pain exploding along her jaw as he wrapped the sash around her face. He pulled it firmly over her mouth. Panic enveloped her. Tossing her head, she staggered sideways, trying to prevent him from cinching the sash. It only made him pull the fabric tighter.

"No!" she cried, but the word was nothing more than a muffled moan.

Breathing heavily through her nose, she tried to kick out again only to be shoved hard against the wall in the corner.

"Enough," he growled.

Adams yanked her to the floor. She closed her eyes, desperately trying to draw sufficient air in through her nose to breathe through the throbbing in her cheek. And then she felt the tug at her ankles and the bite of a cord cutting into her skin. She opened her eyes in time to see Adams step out of the closet and shut the door behind him. The lock clicked, and she was left in complete darkness.

CHAPTER 28

Isabelle rubbed her lips together, the final touches of her makeup now complete. Adrenaline surged through her, the time remaining until she would walk in yet another fashion show quickly pressing in upon her. Unlike the other shows she had been in so far, this time, her schedule had been compressed to uncomfortable levels. Whoever had let the previous show run so late should be fired. Now, here she was with only minutes until she was supposed to walk and she wasn't even dressed yet.

"*Fini*," the makeup artist said as she made the final touches to Isabelle's hair.

"*Merci*." Isabelle stood.

Marit's assistant approached. "Have you seen Marit?"

"Not for a while." Isabelle turned in a circle, searching. "I don't see her anywhere."

Felicia pointed across the backstage area. "Last time I saw her, she was standing over by Chloe."

"I'll keep looking. Thanks." Brookelyn scurried off the way she'd come.

"Who is Chloe?" Isabelle asked. She didn't recall any models or assistants by that name.

"Chloe Brown. She's one of the girls who arrived from New York yesterday."

Isabelle pondered the logic behind bringing in a new model at such a late date. The woman's name wasn't familiar, but Isabelle supposed it was possible that she was in high enough demand that she hadn't been required to go through the fittings and rehearsals. But from what Felicia had said, it sounded like Chloe was one of several.

The fittings. Why would any designer bring in a model without making sure the clothes fit correctly? Unless she had been fitted for her clothes in New York.

The many conversations she'd had with Marit, Cole, and Lars flooded through her mind, and her suspicion heightened. If she was right, they had eliminated some of their suspects prematurely, and these new models were proof that Adams had added new clothes to his line that very well might not be his own.

Needing to run her theory past Marit, Isabelle hurried down the line of stylist stations. She passed by one of the new models as the woman in her early twenties yawned. Judging from the heavy makeup under the woman's eyes and the fatigue in her posture, she had been out far too late last night. Or she had only just arrived in Paris and was fighting jet lag.

Isabelle nearly made it past her dressing area before Hannah, her current assistant, intercepted her. "Hurry. We don't have much time."

Resigned to preparing for the show before speaking to Marit, Isabelle quickly changed out of her clothes and stepped into the floral dress belted at the waist. Hannah zipped her up, and Isabelle leaned down to ease her feet into the white strappy sandals waiting to abuse her blisters.

"Let me help you." Hannah leaned down and buckled the first sandal before quickly moving to buckle the second one.

The moment she was dressed, Isabelle rushed to the backstage area where the other models were lining up.

Someone grabbed Isabelle's arm and guided her to the piece of tape on the floor that marked the twelfth spot, the woman scolding her for being late as she did so. One of the new models took her place two spots up. The presence of several new faces had shifted the walk order around far more drastically than when Camille had swapped her to the number-three spot. Were all the changes due to Adams making room to showcase the designs he had stolen from Ralph?

Isabelle shifted to the side so she could see the front of the line, where Marit would take the third spot in this show, but Marit and the bright-purple jumpsuit were nowhere in sight.

Isabelle checked the time on the clock hanging beside the runway entrance. The show was supposed to have started two minutes ago.

A seed of concern planted inside her. One of the first lessons Marit had taught her was to always be on time. So where was she?

Isabelle turned in a circle, scanning the throngs of people in all directions. One of the new models stepped into the spot Marit was supposed to occupy, her fitted dress one that Isabelle had never seen before.

Every model was in place now except for Marit. Isabelle scanned the area again. Several assistants fiddled with accessories and last-minute adjustments, and Isabelle suddenly realized that Marit wasn't the only person missing. Kyle Adams also wasn't anywhere in sight. The oddity of that ranked right up there with Marit's absence. Every other designer had been beside the staging area long before the models had arrived on their marks.

Isabelle's unease grew, and she stepped out of line.

Olivia, one of Adams's assistants, grabbed her arm. "Where are you going? You go on in four minutes."

"I'll be right back," Isabelle said, not bothering to make up an excuse. She broke free of the woman's grip and hurried to the dressing area assigned to Marit. "Marit?"

No response.

Isabelle pulled aside the curtain. One of Adams's designs hung on the rack, an empty hanger beside it. Marit's clothes were folded neatly on the chair in the corner of the tiny space. Clearly, Marit was already dressed for the show. So where was she? And where was Adams?

Lars adjusted the focus on the camera slung around his neck. He'd chosen to stand to one side of the runway, away from the other photographers and their equipment. He didn't need professional shots of Kyle Adams's new line; he just wanted to blend in.

From this angle, he had a good view of the catwalk and the models as they first stepped under the bright lights. He could also keep an eye on the audience. He wasn't sure what he was looking for exactly. It wasn't as though they were expecting any kind of real threat during Adams's show, but he'd been around Cole enough to know that being alert and observant was always a good thing.

His gaze traversed the front-row seats that ran the length of the runway. Having finished his show, Peter Wade had claimed one of the chairs. Not far from him, a couple of celebrities were seated together, laughing over something. An air of anticipation hovered over the audience, and Lars could only imagine the tension on the other side of the curtain. He fingered the backstage pass lying against his chest, tempted to slip through the curtain to see exactly what was going on. Some candid shots of the hidden frenzy behind the elegance would give people a completely new view of a fashion show.

He pulled his phone from his pocket and glanced at the time just as someone stepped out from between the curtains at the end of the catwalk. The show was about to begin. Abandoning his idea to relocate for the time being, he raised his camera. Marit had told him she would be the third model out, and he didn't want to miss her.

The first model appeared at the head of the catwalk and started her journey down the runway to a ripple of applause. When she reached the bank of photographers at the runway's end, a second model stepped out from between the curtains. Lars kept his eyes on the heavy black fabric. After the second model cleared the way, the curtain twitched, and the third model emerged. Her dark hair was cut short and glistened with gel. Confused, Lars lowered his camera. Marit had told him she was to be the third one out. He was sure of it.

Ignoring the dark-haired model's journey down the runway, he kept his attention on the curtain. The next model appeared. Another stranger. Lars tightened his grip on his camera. What was going on? He was pretty sure Isabelle wasn't scheduled until later in the program, but Marit was one of the industry's lead models. She often opened the shows and rarely started this far down the line.

Lars waited until two more models had walked the length of the runway before acting on his mounting misgivings. Placing his camera in the bag at his feet, he zipped the bag closed, set the strap on his shoulder, and made for the backstage entrance.

The attendant security guard saw him coming and stepped in front of the partition. "Sorry. This is a restricted-access area."

"I know." Lars showed him his pass, offering up silent thanks to the person who'd supplied him and Cole with one.

The guard eyed the backstage pass before grudgingly moving aside. "I hope you know what you're doing," he warned. "It's crazy back there right now."

Crazy enough that Marit would have missed her entrance? Lars didn't think so. Not unless someone or something had prevented her from getting to the curtain.

Grateful that he already had a pretty good idea of the layout backstage, Lars made directly for the area near the front curtain. If Marit had been bumped to a later spot, she'd be standing in line, awaiting her turn. Weaving his way around all the equipment, harried assistants, and tech-support personnel, Lars reached the long queue of models. A few assistants milled around them, straightening sleeves and adjusting collars, but there was no sign of Marit. Come to that, there was no sign of Isabelle either.

Pivoting, Lars headed for the makeup and hair stations. One model was in a chair having pins added to her elaborate hairstyle. Other than her and the waiting stylists, however, the area was empty. After thoroughly scouring the vicinity, he crossed to the changing area.

"Marit?" he called.

He didn't want to pull back the curtains at each cubicle, especially since there may be models using them, but he was getting desperate.

"Marit?" he called again.

"Lars!"

He swung around. Isabelle was hurrying toward him from the area beyond the changing cubicles. She was wearing a floral dress and was moving remarkably quickly given the height of her heels.

"Where's Marit?" Lars asked.

"I was hoping you could tell me." She looked around the cluttered space. "She never showed up at the line. I've searched all the obvious places and haven't found her."

Lars's misgiving was rapidly becoming full-fledged fear. The woman he hoped to marry was in danger. He could sense it. He pulled his phone from his pocket. "Have you called Cole?"

She shook her head. "I was going to get my phone when I heard your voice."

He dialed his cousin's number.

Cole answered on the first ring. "What's going on?"

Was it Lars's imagination, or was Cole out of breath?

"Marit's missing," he said.

"What about Isabelle?"

"She's with me backstage. She doesn't know where Marit is either."

"I'm in the building. I'll be right there." The sound of running footsteps echoed through the phone. "And, Lars, tell Isabelle: Kyle Adams is our man."

CHAPTER 29

Isabelle put her hand on Lars's shoulder, concerned by the way the color had drained from his face. "What did Cole say?"

"He's in the building and headed our way."

"And?"

Lars leaned close and whispered, "He said Adams is our man."

Isabelle had suspected as much, but the confirmation from Cole as well as Marit's absence was enough to push her into action. "I'll check the dressing area again." Isabelle nodded toward the stylist stations. "You check that way."

"Where's Adams?" Lars asked, his hands fisted.

"I haven't seen him, but you need to wait until Cole gets here before we corner him."

Lars swallowed hard. "We have to find her."

"We will." Isabelle started toward the dressing area, but she only made it a few steps before one of Adams's assistants grabbed her by the arm. "Where have you been? You're up next."

"But—"

"No buts." Olivia pulled her toward the runway.

Isabelle looked over her shoulder at Lars, who had already disappeared behind the racks of clothes and the crowd of models waiting to walk.

Isabelle resisted the urge to break Olivia's hold on her. Perhaps Adams's assistant could give her some much-needed information.

"I was looking for Marit," Isabelle asked. "Where is she?"

"She's sick," Olivia said. "Mr. Adams pulled her from the show."

"Mr. Adams told you that?"

"Yes." Olivia continued to propel her forward.

Isabelle reached the opening of the curtain as a panicked assistant waved her forward. "Hurry!"

Even though Isabelle didn't care about Adams's line or his fashion show, the walk down the runway and back would take two minutes tops. It was highly improbable, but maybe Marit was out there. She certainly wasn't backstage.

Isabelle fell into line and moved through the curtains as though she had been waiting her turn the whole time. She scanned the crowd, spotting Peter Wade in the front row. A few other faces were familiar, but Marit wasn't anywhere in sight.

Isabelle pivoted halfway down the runway, her hand on her hip as she did so. She made it to the end and turned, Cole rushing into view as she continued back toward the curtains.

Cole was here. Marit wasn't. Somehow, together they had to find her because there was no doubt Adams was behind the theft of Ralph's designs, *and* it was highly probable that he was also guilty of murder.

If Marit didn't escape before Adams returned, the designer would kill her. It was that simple. And that terrifying. She was simply an expendable pawn in his dangerous and illegal game. Just like Brinton James had been.

Battling the rush of fear that threatened to immobilize her, Marit swallowed against the sash gag. It didn't seem to matter how hard she pulled; her bindings refused to give a millimeter. She'd tried twisting her wrists, but the slight movement had only resulted in the extension cords digging more deeply into her skin. With her arms trapped behind her back, it hadn't taken long for her fingers to start swelling. She flexed them, grateful that they still responded, albeit weakly.

Leaning her head against the closet door, she closed her eyes. She was enveloped in darkness regardless of whether her eyes were open or closed, but closing them helped her pretend that she wasn't locked in a janitorial cupboard. Of course, the pretense would be easier if the smell of cleaning chemicals weren't so potent. Or if her jaw, wrists, and ankles weren't pulsating with pain.

She'd been sitting on the floor ever since Adams had left her, and the intense cold of the floor tiles had long since penetrated the silk jumpsuit she was wearing. The chill was now spreading to the rest of her body. Swinging her knees, she banged them against the door again. There'd been no one in the foyer when Adams had forced her into the closet, but she'd made a concerted effort to hit the door occasionally, not only to signal anyone who may be looking for her but to help keep the blood circulating in her legs.

For at least the hundredth time, she wondered how long it would be before anyone did start looking for her. Cole wasn't even in the building. Isabelle would be racing from the runway to change into her next outfit and then back onto the runway again. She may wonder where Marit was if she didn't see her backstage, but she'd have no time to hunt for her. Lars would notice when she didn't immediately appear on the catwalk, but would he just assume there was a last-minute change in the show's order, or would he go backstage to check on her?

Even if Lars still believed that there was no reason to suspect Adams of any wrongdoing, she didn't think he'd believe the designer if Adams told everyone that Marit had become ill and left. Lars knew Marit would call him if something like that happened. He would try her phone, and if she didn't reply, he'd start searching for her. She knew he would. She could only hope that he would find her before Adams returned.

Cole flashed his badge at the security guard and rushed backstage. He could kick himself for eliminating Adams as a suspect prematurely. He tried to find solace in the fact that he had spoken to Marit only twenty minutes ago, but since she knew about Adams's guilt, it had very likely put her in the danger zone.

He spotted Isabelle exiting the runway and passing through the curtains. Bypassing the dozens of backstage workers, he hurried toward her. "Where's Adams?"

Isabelle looked to her right and then her left before she motioned to an area that was cordoned off. "He's over there, in the backstage viewing area, but he didn't show up there until a few minutes ago."

Cole stepped closer to the area Isabelle indicated so he could get a better look. Several assistants stood beside Adams, a partition at his back and the open space near the front runway area visible through a gap in the curtains. A security guard occupied the open space between the private viewing area and the rest of the backstage space.

Isabelle leaned close. "Do we push past his security to get to him or try to find Marit on our own?"

Cole's instinct was to beat the information out of the smug-looking designer in his tailored suit, but his intelligence training dominated. Demanding information without the right incentive would be counterproductive.

"We need to find Marit," Cole said. Her safety took priority. If anything happened to her, Cole would never forgive himself. Neither would Lars.

That thought had barely formed when Cole spotted his cousin rushing toward him.

"I can't find her anywhere," Lars said.

"Where have you looked?"

"The entire backstage area, except the dressing rooms."

"And I checked those." Isabelle's gaze strayed to an assistant carrying a silver-colored gown. She put one hand on Cole's arm and the other on Lars's, pulling both of them away from the runway entrance and past the dressing rooms. "That's one of Ralph's designs. It's just like one I'm supposed to wear for his show."

"I don't care about the designs," Lars insisted. "We need to find Marit."

"Adams must have taken her somewhere," Isabelle whispered. "He wasn't around when we were first getting ready to start. That's not normal. And he's clearly the person behind the thefts."

Though Cole hated to admit it, the thefts were the least of their concerns. "If we're right, he's already killed for these designs."

Lars's expression went from worried to panicked. "You don't think—"

"She's going to be okay." Cole put his hand on Lars's shoulder. "We'll make sure of it."

"Marit has to be in the building." Isabelle's eyebrows drew together. "There are guards at every exit. Someone would have seen them if Adams or one of his hired hands had taken her outside."

"We need to expand our search." Cole motioned toward the backstage exit. "I'll check with security and have them search their surveillance feed for any sign of Marit. Lars, check the hallways, and, Isabelle, see if any of the other models have seen her."

"What about the police? Shouldn't they be here by now?"

"I don't know. I had Jasmine call them, but I didn't know then that we were dealing with a potential kidnapping scenario." Cole still couldn't quite put together how Adams or anyone else would have managed to tuck Marit out of sight with all these people nearby. "I'll check in with the police when I contact security."

"Make it quick," Lars said.

"I will." Cole squeezed his shoulder. "Keep looking."

CHAPTER 30

Isabelle talked to all the models by the dressing rooms, sidestepping hers for fear that Hannah would try to force her into her next outfit. Isabelle was done with this show, and all she cared about now was stopping Kyle Adams from getting away with theft, fraud, and possibly kidnapping and murder.

Her blood ran cold, and a prayer circled through her head that they would find Marit safe.

Isabelle poked her head between the curtains of the last dressing stall, which the new models were sharing. Several dresses hung on the rack that lined one side of the curtain to her left. Her eyes narrowed. The one in front was one she had seen at the rehearsal for Ralph's show. She stepped deeper into the empty stall and pushed the dress aside. The one behind it also belonged to Ralph Molenaar's collection. She checked the other two dresses, both of them familiar.

Isabelle snatched all four dresses off the rack. These were supposed to be in the finale for Ralph's shows. She may not have found Marit yet, but she could at least prevent Adams from claiming these few gowns.

Cautiously, Isabelle peeked through the curtains. Two assistants waited just outside, their attention on the curtains near the end of the runway. Hannah approached them, a frantic look on her face. No doubt, she was looking for Isabelle.

Isabelle stepped out of the dressing stall and headed away from the runway entrance, using the dressing rooms to hide her from view.

She scanned the area for a place to hide the dresses as well as for anywhere she and Lars may have missed where Marit could be tucked away. They had looked in every dressing room, shipping container, and stylist station in the backstage area without luck. Cole was right. They needed to expand their search.

Isabelle strode to the heavy black curtains that hung off the partitions that created the backstage area. Shifting the gowns over one arm, she bent down and lifted the closest curtain. She then stepped behind it, the heavy fabric trapping her between it and the partition.

Ready to rid herself of the burden of the dresses, she reached up and hooked the hangers over the top of the partition. With the wall directly behind it, the tops of the hangers should remain hidden from view, and the curtains would keep them invisible to anyone in the backstage area.

Invisible. Could Marit be as close as the space between the curtains and partitions? Placing one hand on the partition, Isabelle moved steadily forward.

Cole's phone call to Capitaine Dupont had revealed that the capitaine and Brigadier Blanchet were still fighting their way through traffic from across town, and now Cole had to deal with a group of security guards who were more concerned about crowd control and protecting clothing than they were about finding Marit.

Cole balled his hands into fists and stepped closer to the head of security. "Did you not understand what I said? A woman is missing. It's possible the man responsible for a murder last week is to blame."

"I understand, monsieur, and we will look into it as soon as we can."

As soon as they could. This was why Cole preferred to take care of matters himself.

Impatient, he motioned to the surveillance cameras. "All I'm asking is for you to review the security feed from 18:45 to 19:10. Marit disappeared sometime during that window, probably closer to the beginning of it. And I need some security guards to help us look."

"I don't have enough staff to search, not while the show is going on, but we'll check with our guards to see if anyone saw anything unusual."

"But—"

Before Cole could voice his objection, the security chief added, "I'll put a man on the surveillance feed." He called out to a man at the bank of screens and spoke in French. The man nodded and moved to a computer station at the end of the long desk.

Satisfied that his orders had been followed, the head of security turned back to Cole. "Marquis will conduct a search."

Even though Cole wanted far more assistance than he was getting, he said, "*Merci.*" He eyed the bank of screens on the wall. "How many cameras do you have near the fashion shows?"

"Fourteen."

Fourteen. Even using fast-forward, this could take a while. "Let me give you my phone number." After the security chief handed him a piece of paper and a pen, he jotted it down. "I'm going to help my friends with the search."

"I'll call you if my people find anything."

Cole nodded and left the security office. He pulled out his phone and dialed Capitaine Dupont's number.

The man answered a moment later.

Cole identified himself and asked, "How close are you?"

"We'll be there in five minutes."

"Hurry. We still haven't found Marit Jansen."

"We're on our way."

CHAPTER 31

Lars reemerged from the makeup area, panic pulsing through his veins. Marit wasn't there. He'd known it after the first time he'd checked, but he'd run out of places to look for her, and desperation was making him second-guess everything. He stopped, forcing himself to think past his fears. There had to be somewhere he'd missed. He didn't believe for one minute that she'd gone back to the flat or even to a nurse's station within the building. If she'd really taken ill, she would have called him or told Isabelle before she'd left.

Two assistants hurried past, carrying clothes toward the changing rooms. Isabelle had gone to check that area. He trusted her to do a thorough job, and she hadn't emerged from there yet. Moving quickly, he cut around the assistants, heading directly for the changing area. He caught movement at his left and glanced that way in time to see Isabelle slip out from between the black curtains behind the changing rooms. Veering that direction, he came up beside her.

"Anything?" he asked.

"No," she said. "I found her clothes, so she's wearing one of Adams's outfits. Probably the purple jumpsuit."

Lars didn't care what Marit was wearing. He just wanted to find her.

"What's behind the black curtain?"

"There's a narrow gap between the curtain and the partition that cordons off this part of the museum."

It was somewhere new to search, and Lars seized on it. "How far down did you go?"

"I checked the section behind the changing area."

He was already heading toward the break in the curtain. "I'll continue left if you'll see how much farther it goes on the right."

Isabelle nodded. "I'll meet you back here afterward."

The black curtain was heavy, and the moment Lars stepped behind it, his visibility dropped. Faint light filtered in from above the top of the partition, but it was barely enough to pick out the large extension cords running across the floor. Deciding that the risk of his phone light being seen through the curtain was less than his risk of tripping and bringing the curtain down around him, he turned the light on. The bright light illuminated a meter or two ahead of him. Three cables and the bulky base of the curtain's metal frame lay across the floor ahead of him. He released a tense breath. It was a good thing he'd turned on the light.

Stepping over the obstacles, he continued forward, moving as quickly as he dared. Another few meters and the darkness eased a fraction. Lowering his phone, he moved closer. There appeared to be a break in the partition. He slowed his pace, approaching the gap cautiously even as he attempted to picture exactly where he was on the Louvre's floor plan. The main entrance to the fashion show would be on the opposite side, which meant that security would be tightest over there, but this area would undoubtedly be blocked off. There may not be anything of interest to the public back here, but they'd want to prevent anyone from accessing backstage.

He peered around the partition. Sure enough, the hall beyond was completely empty. He stepped into it, glancing up and down. No sign of security. But no sign of anyone else either. A sign on the wall at his right caught his attention. Toilets. Crossing the short distance at a run, he darted into the men's toilets. The entire place was empty. He exited and eyed the ladies' toilets. If anyone other than Marit was inside, he'd apologize later.

"Coming in!" he yelled, bursting into the tiled room. A row of sinks faced a row of toilet stalls. "Marit!"

He was met by silence. Walking along the length of the room, he pushed open each stall door. No one. And no sign of anyone having been there for some time. These toilets probably hadn't been used since the Fashion Week props and equipment had been installed.

Hurrying out, he paused in the middle of the hall to scan the area again. "Where are you, Marit?"

Desperation was threatening to consume him, but the only response to his muttered question was a faint thud from somewhere nearby. Clenching his fists, Lars attempted to push past his panic. Was it worth his time to go any farther down the hall? And if so, which way? The faint thud sounded again. The thick curtain muted all the backstage noises, but the thud hadn't seemed to be coming from there. It had come from his left. He started in that direction. Another thud. It was coming from behind a door labeled Janitor's Cupboard.

In three seconds, he'd reached the door. Grabbing the handle, he attempted to turn it. It was locked.

"Marit. Are you in there?"

Three more thuds vibrated through the wood. Lars's heart began to pound. If she wasn't responding verbally, she must be gagged. He had to get the door open. Fast. His mind raced. Who would have a key? Or who could get in without one?

"Hang on, Marit!" His voice was low, urgent. He couldn't risk anyone else hearing him, but he hoped she could. "I'm going for help."

Tearing across the hall, he slid through the gap in the partition. Directly in front of him was a break in the dark curtain. With a level of caution he wished he could ignore, he carefully eased the fabric back a few centimeters. A quick look into the backstage area told him that the show was still in full swing. Blending into the chaos would be easy enough. He stepped through the curtain and had only taken three steps when he heard Isabelle's voice.

"Lars! Over here."

He swung around. She was standing partially hidden behind another curtain.

"My assistant's looking for me," she said. "Standing in the changing area wasn't an option."

"Good thinking," Lars said. "We've got more important things to deal with. I think I've found Marit, but I need Cole to get her out of a locked closet."

"Cole's not back yet." She glanced at the cluster of assistants standing at the nearest clothing rack. "But if you can get me a metal nail file from one of the makeup stations, I can open it."

Lars didn't question her. He made directly for the closest table. Three makeup artists were talking together a couple of meters away. Offering up a silent prayer that none of them would look his way, he eyed the rows of brushes, bottles, tubes, powders, and swabs. There had to be a nail file among all this stuff. He glanced over his shoulder. No one had noticed him yet. Shifting a jar full of brushes, he reached for one filled with small utensils. Tweezers, nail scissors, clippers. Finally. A nail file. Pulling it out of the jar, he took off the way he'd come.

Isabelle must have been watching for him. She was already slipping through the curtain when he reached her hiding spot. Together they crept behind the partition and down the hall.

"Right there," he said as they passed the bathrooms, handing her the nail file and pointing to the janitor's cupboard.

She ran across the hall, and within seconds, she was on her knees, pressing the nail file into the gap between the door and the frame. There was another thud, and the door vibrated.

"Hang on, Marit." Like Lars, Isabelle kept her voice low, her concentration fully on the lock. She shifted her wrist a fraction. "I've almost got it."

Keeping the nail file in place with one hand, she lifted the other to the doorknob and pulled. She scrambled to her feet as Lars reached for the door and drew it open. Marit was sitting on the floor, her knees pulled up, her ankles bound. Her arms were pulled back behind her, and a purple sash was tied around her mouth. She was squinting, blinking against the light. But she was alive.

Relief swept over Lars in a tidal wave only to be replaced moments later by a surge of fury at the man behind this despicable act. He reached around Marit's head, tugging at the knot that bound her gag tight. She closed her eyes and moaned. He eased his frantic movements, drawing one end of the sash through the knot more gently.

"I'm so sorry, Marit." His emotions swirled. He didn't know what he wanted most: to wrap Marit in his arms or to take down Adams.

Vaguely aware that Isabelle was working to release Marit's ankles, Lars loosened the gag enough to pull it free from Marit's mouth. She gasped as though taking in air for the first time after having been underwater.

"I prayed you would come." Her voice was little more than a whisper.

"She needs water," Isabelle said.

Lars scoured the shelves behind them. Toilet paper, paper towels, plastic bags, cleaning supplies. No cups. With fumbling fingers, he separated the two ends of the sash and pulled it free from Marit's neck. "Give me ten seconds," he said.

He ran into the men's toilets, turned on the closest sink, and dunked the sash under the tap. When the fabric was completely saturated, he turned off the tap and raced back to the janitor's closet. Isabelle had freed Marit's feet and was now working on her wrists. Lars knelt down beside his girlfriend and lifted the sodden fabric to her mouth. Drips of water ran down his arms and fell to the floor.

"It's not a cup," he said, "but it's wet. Maybe it will help."

Marit opened her mouth to accept the wet fabric. She sucked some of the moisture out before swallowing, her expression indicating that the simple action was painful.

"Who was it?" Isabelle asked.

Marit drew her hands out from behind her back. Her wrists were raw and bleeding. Softly, Lars placed the wet cloth on them.

"Kyle Adams," Marit said.

"Where's Cole?" Lars asked, doing nothing to hide the anger in his voice. "It's time to go after Adams."

"He hasn't gotten back from talking to security." Isabelle looked over her shoulder. "He should be here any minute."

Leaving the wet cloth draped across Marit's wrists, Lars leaned forward and cupped her face gently in his hand. "I'm going to find Cole and update security about what's happened. I promise you, Adams won't be walking out of here a free man." Knowing that she was too fragile to be kissed the way he wanted to kiss her, he pressed his lips to her forehead. "I'll be back as fast as I can."

"It . . ." Marit swallowed and winced. "It might take me a few minutes before I'm up for walking, but if Isabelle's here, I'll be okay."

Lars looked at Isabelle.

She nodded. "I've got this. Go find Cole."

CHAPTER 32

Marit lifted the wet sash from her injured wrists to dab at the cuts on her ankles. Drops of blood mingled with the water that dripped onto the exorbitantly priced silk jumpsuit she was wearing. Under normal circumstances, she would have been horrified. Now she glanced at the stains numbly.

Kyle Adams had done this to her. And he'd likely planned to do far worse once the show was over. The show. She gasped. It was the first time she'd thought of it since hearing Lars's voice on the other side of the closet door.

"Isabelle! We have to stop the show. Adams has made replicas of Ralph's designs and plans to use them in his finale."

"I know," Isabelle said grimly. "I spotted them when we were looking for you."

Marit set one hand on the floor to push herself to her feet. Pain radiated upward from her wrists, and her arm trembled. She rotated slightly, attempting to distribute her weight more evenly. "We have to get in there."

"We have to do a couple other things first," Isabelle said, reaching down to help her up.

"We don't have time."

"I bought us a little time. I hid the copied gowns Adams was planning to put in his finale. He's going to be frantic, trying to find them before the show ends." Isabelle helped her stumble to her feet. "And taking care of you needs to be our priority right now. First, we have to make sure you can stand alone, and second, we need to put Band-Aids on the worst of your cuts."

"I don't care how much blood gets on Adams's outfit," Marit said, leaning against the wall while she gave her throbbing ankles time to adjust to her upright position.

"Neither do I." Cautiously, Isabelle released her hold on Marit's arm and stepped back. "But everyone backstage will, and you'll be mobbed by well-meaning assistants if you reappear bleeding like that."

Which would make accessing the runway entrance and the general manager all but impossible. The words went unspoken, but Marit knew she couldn't risk drawing the attention of Adams before she spoke to someone in authority over running the show.

"My left wrist is the worst," Marit said. "Maybe I can cover that with the sash."

Isabelle shook her head. "I have a whole box of bandages in my purse." She glanced up and down the empty hall. "If you think you'll be okay for a minute, I'll run and grab them."

"I'll be fine." She took a small step away from the wall. Already, the unsteadiness in her legs was improving. "Go now. We have to be getting close to the finale."

Isabelle didn't hesitate. She ran across the hall and disappeared between the gap in the partition.

Marit released a tight breath and took another small step. The movement pulled at the damaged skin on her right ankle, but she resisted the urge to limp. If she was going to stop the show, she was going to have to ignore the pain.

Staying close to the wall, she managed another three steps, then she retraced them back to the cupboard entrance. She picked up the wet sash that she'd left on the floor and wiped a fresh trickle of blood off her left arm. Hurried footsteps sounded behind her.

"That was fast." Marit turned around.

"Not fast enough, apparently." Adams drew his gun from his pocket. "How did your friend unlock the door? And where did you hide the clothes?"

Marit dropped the sash to the floor. The trembling returned to her limbs, but she refused to allow Adams to see it. She also wasn't going to tell him how she'd escaped. If he knew that three people—maybe more, if Cole and Lars had spoken with security by now—knew exactly where she was and what he'd done, there was no accounting for what he might do now.

She leaned against the wall, grateful for its stability. "I don't know the answers to either of those questions."

"Don't lie to me," he snarled.

"I'm not lying."

He took another menacing step toward her, and for a fleeting moment, Marit considered backing into the closet and closing the door between them. It wouldn't stop Adams for long, but it might buy her friends time to get back.

"I'm only going to ask you this one more time." Adams's eyes flashed, and he raised his gun a little higher. "Where did you put the clothes?"

Get out of the line of fire. Stay out of the line of fire. Unbidden, Cole's instructions flashed into her mind. Marit had truly hoped she would never again face a weapon, but Cole had told her what she needed to do. She pressed her hand against the wall. She didn't feel ready. The closet would be easier. Unfortunately, it would also trap her completely. She couldn't risk having Adams do to her what he'd done to James.

Her heart racing, she took a step toward Adams. "The only clothes I know anything about are the ones I'm wearing."

"Where are the blue, silver, and gold gowns?" he hissed. "When the pink trouser suit didn't come out on schedule, I knew exactly who to blame. But you're not going to prevent me from showing those gowns." He narrowed his eyes. "You have three seconds to tell me where they are."

Pushing herself into motion, Marit struck her right hand out, grabbing at Adams's wrist with as much force as she could muster.

Shock flashed across his face. His grip loosened, and the gun went flying out of his hand.

Isabelle stepped into the hall at the same moment a gun skidded across the floor and thudded against the wall. It came to a stop midway between where Adams and Marit stood and where Isabelle had entered.

Isabelle's shock at finding him here, armed and away from the stage, mirrored the expression on Adams's face.

Marit and Adams scrambled toward the gun as Isabelle rushed forward. Adams was faster.

He leaned down to retrieve the weapon when Isabelle was still two steps away.

"Watch out!" Marit cried.

Clearly determined to keep the pistol out of Adams's possession, Marit thrust both arms out to keep him from reaching the gun. She succeeded in pushing him off-balance, and Isabelle kicked her leg out, her stiletto heel clipping his arm.

The force of impact knocked him back another step and prevented him from retrieving the gun that was currently between his feet.

He reached down again, but this time, Isabelle was close enough to use her hands. She took a quick step forward and thrust her arm out, the heel of her hand striking Adams in the chin.

His head jolted back; the force of the open-palm strike sent him stumbling once more but not enough to give Isabelle or Marit the space needed to grab the weapon without risking a kick to the head.

Adams recovered more quickly than Isabelle had expected, and fury flashed in his eyes. "You don't know who you're dealing with. I'll kill you both."

"Just like you killed Brinton James?" Isabelle asked.

Adams's only response was to dive for his weapon. Before he could reach it, Isabelle kicked it and sent it sliding out of reach.

"Marit, grab the gun!"

Marit hobbled toward it, but again, Adams was faster. He rushed forward, leaned down to pick it up, and Isabelle launched herself at him, grabbing Adams from behind.

He straightened, pistol in hand, and turned quickly, Isabelle now clinging to his back.

"Marit, get down!"

Marit darted into the closet an instant before a gunshot sparked through the air. The bullet thudded into the doorframe right beside where Marit had been standing only a second earlier.

Isabelle hooked her arm around Adams's throat, pressing on his windpipe with the crook of her elbow.

Adams turned in a circle, reaching back with his free hand to grab at Isabelle. When his efforts proved unsuccessful, he swiveled and rammed Isabelle into the wall.

Pain shot through her shoulder, which had absorbed most of the impact, and a moan escaped her.

Isabelle's hold loosened, and Adams broke free. He whirled, aiming his gun at the same time Marit burst back out of the closet wielding a broom.

Marit swung the broom at Adams's legs. Wood cracked against his knee.

Adams cried out.

Isabelle pushed his arm to the side, taking herself out of the line of fire. She used her free hand to twist his wrist backward. The pistol discharged again, the bullet shattering the tile and sending bits of porcelain flying into the air.

Isabelle used her weight and all her strength to slam Adams's arm against the wall.

He grunted in pain, but the gun remained firmly in his grip.

Marit swung the broom again, this time at Adams's back. Clearly stunned, Adams's fingers opened. The gun dropped onto his shoe, then tumbled back to the floor.

Isabelle kicked it, sending it toward Marit.

Adams turned to chase after the gun, but Isabelle blocked his path. Before he could take more than a step, Marit scooped up the weapon and aimed it at him.

"Stop right there!" Marit demanded, her voice trembling slightly.

Adams stopped, his hands out to his sides. He looked at Marit, glanced at Isabelle, and then faced Marit once more.

Desperation flashed in his eyes, the kind that warned Isabelle that he wasn't going to simply surrender.

Frantic for anything she could use as a weapon, she reached down and slid a high heel off one of her feet. She hurled the shoe at Adams's head at the same time he rushed toward Marit.

He must have seen it coming, because he ducked, but the distraction was enough for Isabelle to close the distance between them.

The curtains opened, and Cole rushed in, his gun drawn. Before he could act, Isabelle struck her hand out again, palm first. The blow landed on Adams's chin, and his head jerked back.

An instant later, Marit slammed the gun, butt first, against his head.

Adams moaned in pain and crumpled to the floor.

"Don't move!" Cole aimed his weapon at Adams, but this time, Adams didn't attempt to rise. Cole glanced at Isabelle. "Are you all right?"

"Other than my blister ripping open again, I'm fine."

Two police officers entered the hall. Lars followed.

"That's him." Cole pointed at Adams. "He's the one behind the Molenaar theft."

"And a kidnapping," Marit added. In an instant, Lars was at her side, his arms wrapping firmly around her.

"Cuff him," the older of the two men ordered.

The younger one hauled Adams to his feet and cuffed his hands behind his back.

"This is his weapon." Marit handed the pistol to the officer closest to her.

Cole nodded his approval. "If we're right about him, the ballistics will match the gun that killed James and Bernard."

"We'll run the tests," the older officer said.

"Thank you, Capitaine Dupont and Brigadier Blanchet." Cole holstered his weapon and moved to Isabelle's side.

"We need to take your statements," Brigadier Blanchet said. "Would you prefer to do that here or at the station?"

"Here," Isabelle said without hesitation.

"We'll take care of that as soon as we secure the prisoner," Capitaine Dupont said.

"Thanks," Cole said. "And please keep me in the loop."

"We'll call you when the ballistic reports come back."

"*Merci.*"

The officers escorted their prisoner away.

Taking advantage of Cole's nearness, Isabelle put her arm around his waist, grateful when he drew her closer. "Thank goodness that's over."

"Not quite." Marit shot her a look of determination. "There's one more thing we need to do." She turned to Lars. "You should go back into the photographers' area. You won't want to miss this."

Lars loosened his hold on her enough to see her face. "Miss what?"

Marit glanced at Isabelle briefly before she said, "It's time for everyone out there to know the truth."

CHAPTER 33

Limping slightly, Marit cut through the gap in the partition and entered the backstage area with Isabelle at her side. There were at least a dozen models in line. Most of them were wearing Adams's designs, though a couple of them wore Ralph Molenaar's.

Three of the American models stood off to one side, their assistants hovering nearby. If the strained look on each of the assistants' faces was any indication, they had yet to locate the dresses Isabelle had hidden away. Marit mentally applauded Isabelle's quick thinking. It would enable Ralph to use those pieces in his show tomorrow. She eyed the stage director standing at the curtain. If her plan worked, Ralph could use the ones that had already been showcased, too, but that decision would be up to him.

"The director's going to do everything in her power to prevent me from going out there," Marit spoke softly.

"Oh, I know." Isabelle appeared completely unruffled. "But it won't be a problem."

Marit smothered a grin. Together, she and Isabelle had just battled and disarmed a gunman. The poor woman with the clipboard didn't stand a chance.

"Glad you're on my side," Marit said.

This time, Isabelle smiled. "Me too."

As they walked past the waiting models, heads turned and whispers ran along the length of the line.

"You're causing a stir," Isabelle said.

"Yeah. The blood on Adams's jumpsuit is not going to be well-received."

Isabelle frowned. "If that's all they care about, you should change professions."

"Probably," Marit said, "but right now, I'm going to make use of it in the best possible way." She glanced at Isabelle. "Ready?"

"Absolutely. I'll take care of everything back here; the stage is yours."

Marit's pulse quickened. Though she was well used to walking the runway, making a public announcement was out of her comfort zone. But it had to be done. Adams needed to be exposed, and Ralph deserved credit for his creations.

"Miss Jansen." They'd reached the curtain, and the stage director was studying the purple jumpsuit with a horrified expression. "I hope you have a good explanation for the state of this outfit and your absence when the show began."

"I do," Marit said.

Another model appeared through the curtain, her time on the catwalk over. The director gestured at the first model in line, but before the young woman wearing an oversized lacy blouse and leather trousers could take a step toward the stage, Isabelle moved in front of her.

"You're going to have to wait," Isabelle said. "Marit's going first."

The model gave the director a frantic look, and the woman turned her glare on Isabelle.

"What do you think you're doing?"

Marit didn't wait to hear Isabelle's response. With the stage director's attention diverted, she slipped through the curtain and onto the runway.

The spotlight hit her immediately. Ignoring her instinct to start down the catwalk, she glanced to her right, catching sight of the microphone used to introduce the designer and his team at the end of the show. In three limping steps, she crossed the distance and tugged the microphone off the stand.

The only model left on the runway approached the curtain. Giving Marit an uncertain look, she disappeared backstage.

Marit started down the runway, her uneven gait a stark contrast to her normally fluid movement. Shocked whispers followed her, and she heard the chorus of camera clicks as she approached the photographers lining the catwalk. All being well, Lars was among them. He'd know exactly what needed to be documented.

She raised the microphone to her mouth. "Ladies and gentlemen," she began, "I regret to inform you that several of the outfits showcased this evening were not Kyle Adams originals. The designs were stolen from Ralph Molenaar's collection. Mr. Adams has been taken into police custody, and the remainder of this show has been canceled."

In the audience, the slight murmur that had begun when Marit had first appeared became an indignant rumble.

Alongside the catwalk, Peter Wade leaped to his feet. "I knew it! Those denim overalls were a signature Molenaar creation."

All around the room, people were rising. A couple of cameramen jumped onto the end of the catwalk, turning their cameras on the indignant crowd. Near the exits, security guards and police officers were filtering in, taking positions around the room as the show's shocked attendees began to move. Almost everyone held a mobile phone, and those who weren't taking pictures or typing messages were making calls.

Lowering the microphone in her hand, Marit released an unsteady breath. Her job was done. Social media and the official news outlets would take over from here.

Cole let himself into Marit and Isabelle's flat, his limbs heavy with fatigue. He'd been torn between going to the police station and staying with Isabelle, Marit, and Lars after Marit had put a stop to Kyle Adams's show. Ultimately, he had opted to get answers firsthand by accompanying Capitaine Dupont and Brigadier Blanchet to the police station so he could observe their interrogation.

Cole had to admit, Adams did a pretty good job spinning his story to make it look like Isabelle and Marit had tried to undermine him. Ultimately, the ballistics report had ended the interrogation and Adams's willingness to answer questions. The gun Adams had pulled on Marit was the weapon used to murder James and Bernard.

Cole closed and bolted the door to the flat behind him and flipped on the light.

Across the room, Isabelle lay on the shorter of the two couches. She squinted and cracked both eyes open.

Cole crossed the room so his voice wouldn't wake Lars or Marit, both of whom he assumed were sleeping in their respective bedrooms. "What are you doing out here?"

"Waiting for you." She swung her legs over the edge of the couch and sat up. "What happened at the police station?"

"Adams claimed that you and Marit were stealing his clothes and trying to undermine his show."

"The police didn't buy that, did they?"

"No." Cole dropped onto the couch beside her. "The abrasions on Marit's ankles and wrists made it pretty obvious that Marit's story was the accurate one. And the ballistic report confirmed the gun was the same one used to kill both James and Bernard."

"Did he confess?"

"No, but with the financial records the CIA sent over and Marit's testimony, the case against him is pretty strong." Cole rolled his head from one side to the other in an attempt to relieve the stiffness that had settled there. "He's going to prison one way or another."

"That's good news." Isabelle put her hand on Cole's shoulder. "Here. Let me give you a shoulder rub."

Cole shifted to give her easier access to his back, and Isabelle put both hands on his shoulders. She kneaded at the tight muscles there.

"I talked to Marit about skipping the LaRue show on Saturday, but she's determined that we need to be there."

"Why?" Cole asked. "Between the blisters on your feet and how raw her wrists and ankles are, I'm not sure a couple days off will be enough to heal."

"I know, but she thinks that if people see her on the runway, it will keep them talking about tonight's show and what Adams tried to do to Ralph."

"Marit does have a strong sense of right and wrong."

"Yes, she does. She also handled herself remarkably well when we faced off against Adams." Isabelle continued to massage his shoulders, and Cole hummed his approval.

"If it weren't for the fact that Lars would kill me, I'd seriously consider recruiting her," Cole said.

"I had the same thought." Isabelle moved her hands from his shoulders to his neck, pressing her thumbs against a particularly tight spot.

The worst of the tension left his body, and Cole let his head fall forward. "I really love you right now."

Isabelle's fingers stilled. "Right now?"

Cole's words caught up with him. Had he really just said the *L* word? He straightened and turned to face her, sheer panic streaking through him.

Would admitting his feelings scare her off? Or would it complicate their relationship?

The vulnerability in her expression pushed him to share the truth he had kept buried since the moment he'd discovered his true feelings. "Not just right now." He forced his gaze to meet hers. "I always love you."

Isabelle blinked twice, as though not sure if she was awake or dreaming. "Really?"

Her dazed expression gave him hope that his feelings weren't one-sided. "Yes, really."

Unable to resist, he lifted both hands to her cheeks and leaned in until his lips met hers. The familiar spark ignited between them, and his heart swelled. Isabelle settled her hand on his shoulder, and he indulged himself by deepening the kiss.

For so long, his focus had been on the next mission, on simply staying alive. With his lips warm on Isabelle's, he now knew that there was more to living than simply keeping his heart beating.

His fingers slid into her hair, the silky strands brushing against his skin. He changed the angle of the kiss, and his love for Isabelle flowed into it.

When he drew back, he kept his face close to hers. "Is this too fast for you?" he asked. "I can pretend I never said I love you."

Isabelle shook her head, her eyes fixing on his. "It's not too fast, because I love you too."

Pure joy filled him, and he leaned in for another kiss. "I'm really glad you came to Paris."

"Me too."

CHAPTER 34

Isabelle felt like a princess. Her silver Ralph Molenaar gown flowed down to the floor, and her hair was teased into a sophisticated updo. The diamond necklace and earrings she wore cost more than her annual salary, which was evidenced by the guards standing at the far end of the runway and backstage.

Cole had taken position opposite the backstage security guard, his weapon hidden beneath his suit jacket.

She caught his gaze out of the corner of her eye, and he winked at her.

The smile she had pasted on for the cameras widened. She still couldn't believe Cole had declared his love, especially in such an unexpected way, or how those three little words had become such a common phrase between them over the past five days.

Beside her, Marit turned her head slightly, no doubt to find Lars in the photographer's area. The love between the two was palpable, but the little seed of envy Isabelle had experienced when she'd first arrived in Paris had died, leaving only happiness for herself and her friend.

Lars took several shots of Marit, Isabelle, and Nadia before redirecting his camera toward the three models mirroring their position on the other side of the runway entrance.

Lars had barely lowered his camera when Ralph stepped through the curtains and took his place beside Marit.

Applause erupted, the crowd coming to their feet.

Ralph bowed, and the applause only increased. He waved one hand toward the models on his right and then repeated the gesture toward Marit, Isabelle, and Nadia.

After bowing a second time, he lifted a hand in the air to acknowledge the crowd and stepped back through the curtains. Isabelle fell in line as the models filed off the runway and into the backstage area.

Cole appeared at her side an instant later. So did the security guard.

"Mademoiselles, please wait here while we collect the jewelry," the guard said.

"Better wait for Lars," Cole said.

Lars approached before the guard had a chance to respond. Apparently, he wasn't willing to walk around to the backstage entrance, instead following the models' path through the curtains.

"Let me photograph the pieces as we pack them," Lars instructed the guard.

One by one, the models removed their necklaces, earrings, and bracelets, Lars documenting each piece with his camera.

As soon as Isabelle handed over the pieces adorning her neck and ears, she placed her hand on Cole's arm. "I'm going to change."

Cole nodded. "I'll meet you by those cubbies where you left your purse."

"It's not my purse," Isabelle said. "I need to return it to Ralph."

"We can take care of that before we leave." Cole leaned in and kissed her cheek. "See you in a few minutes."

Isabelle nodded.

Marit stepped up beside her. "I'll come with you."

The two made their way to the dressing rooms and changed into their regular clothes. Isabelle set her high heels on the rack and took her time to pull on her favorite sneakers.

Relieved that her blisters had healed significantly over the past few days, she stepped out of her changing room and found Marit waiting for her.

"I can't believe I'm finally finished." Isabelle let out a sigh of relief. "My modeling career is over."

"Maybe," Marit said. "If Esmee has her way, this is only the beginning."

"That's sweet of her to think I can be successful at this, but from now on, I'm leaving the modeling to you. It's way too much work for me."

Marit laughed. "Come on. Let's find our boyfriends."

Isabelle led the way to the cubbies and retrieved the bag that she and Marit had been sharing since Marit's was stolen. "We need to find something to put our stuff in so we can return this purse to Ralph."

"I'll bet he has a bag or box we can use." Marit headed toward where Ralph was standing with several of his assistants, an air of celebration sparking in the air.

"Sorry to interrupt," Marit said, stepping beside Ralph. "Do you have something we can put our stuff in so we can return your bag to you?"

Ralph shook his head. "I want you to keep it."

"Oh, we couldn't possibly—" Marit began.

"Of course you can. Without you and your friends, my company would have been ruined." He motioned to one of his assistants. "Where's the other one?"

"Right here." The woman picked up another purse he had designed.

"I'll let the two of you decide who wants which one," Ralph said.

"You really don't have to do that," Isabelle said.

"It's a small token of my appreciation," Ralph said. "Truly, thank you."

"You're welcome." Marit accepted the second bag from the assistant.

A reporter approached Ralph, pulling him away.

"That was very kind of him," Isabelle said.

"It really was," Marit agreed. "You know what I think?"

"What?"

"You and Cole need to stay through the weekend, and we need to have the guys take us out where we can enjoy having these great new bags."

"As long as I don't have to put on another pair of heels, that sounds like a fabulous idea."

CHAPTER 35

THE SUN WAS SHINING, CHASING away the morning chill as Lars and Marit followed behind Cole and Isabelle along the narrow streets of Montmartre. They walked through a picturesque, cobbled square, and Lars slid his arm more securely around Marit's waist, love for the beautiful woman beside him swelling in his chest. She glanced at him and smiled. Lars responded by dropping a gentle kiss on her cheek. As soon as they were back in Amsterdam, he was going to put a rush job on the diamond ring he hoped to put on her finger.

"I love you," he whispered.

The look in her eyes softened. "I love you too."

"This is what spending time in Paris with your girlfriend is supposed to be like, you know." He glanced around. "Walking arm in arm through historic districts filled with quaint cafés and flower markets."

She laughed softly. "We didn't do it right last week, did we?"

"Not even remotely."

"Since the police have wrapped up their questioning, all the fashion shows are over, and the Coster diamonds are safely on their way back to Amsterdam, I think today's going to be much better."

Lars really hoped Marit was right. "Pretty sure we're all overdue for 'much better,'" he said.

"Yeah." Marit's gaze shifted to Cole and Isabelle, who were walking hand in hand a couple of meters ahead of them. "We are."

As if he'd sensed their attention on him, Cole turned. "Are you guys up for going as far as Sacré Cœur?"

Lars fingered the camera slung around his neck. He'd already taken some great photos of the Montmartre neighborhoods, but he'd love to take some of the famous basilica. "How far is it?" he asked.

"About half a mile, I think."

"If Isabelle can manage it with her healing blisters, we can too," Marit said.

"Especially if we stop at a pâtisserie on the way back," Lars added.

"Deal," Cole said. He didn't appear to need much persuading. They'd passed several pâtisseries already, and it seemed to Lars that Cole's feet had slowed outside each one.

Isabelle pointed to the right. "The sign on the wall over there says that Sacré Cœur is this way."

"Okay," Cole said. "Let's go. I've heard about the stained-glass windows inside, but I've never actually seen them."

They turned the corner. The road ahead rose steeply, bending to the left at the base of a steep set of stairs. They kept walking, and the closer they drew to the stairs, the steeper they appeared.

"Where do those go?" Lars asked.

"If the signs are to be believed," Isabelle said, "they lead to Sacré Cœur."

"Seriously?"

"Yep." Cole confirmed.

Lars didn't know what it was about stairs. He just knew that he hated them. "It's too early in the day for that many stairs," he said.

With a laugh, Marit took his hand. "Come on, we've got this."

Lars sighed. Marit and Isabelle both had enough stairs leading to their respective flats that they were completely unfazed by these. Cole was just crazy enough to take them two at a time.

Even though Cole climbed the stairs slower than usual, he reached the top a couple of steps ahead of Lars. "Uh-oh," Cole said.

Joining him on the pavement, Lars eyed him warily. "I don't like the sound of that."

Cole gestured across the street. "You're not going to like the look of that either."

Lars swung around. Directly in front of him and across the road was another set of steep staircases. And immediately above that was yet another set. "Are you kidding me?" Lars asked.

Cole raised an eyebrow. "You did want to visit Sacré Cœur."

"Not at the risk of being unable to use my legs for the rest of the day."

"To be fair, I didn't know it was stairs the whole way," Isabelle said. "But I'm pretty sure this means you get to buy more than one item from the pâtisserie afterward."

"And we're more prepared than you thought." Marit swung her new Ralph Molenaar purse around so it was clearly visible. "Isabelle and I have purses to carry the extras in."

Despite his dread of the hike ahead, Lars grinned. "We should probably make a pact of secrecy right now. No one is to tell Ralph if we put éclairs and mille feuille inside them."

"Mille feuille might be pushing it a bit," Isabelle said, a hint of concern in her voice. "They're not exactly self-contained."

"Okay, I'll eat the mille feuille before we leave the pâtisserie," Lars said.

"I'm taking that as your agreement to tackle the stairs," Cole said. "Let's go."

Eight minutes and four double flights of stairs later, they reached the top. By the time they'd climbed the third set, Lars had decided that breathing normally was better than anything he could buy at the pâtisserie. He'd now reached the point where he was pretty sure he'd have to live out the rest of his life at the top of Montmartre.

"There's no way every visitor to Sacré Cœur climbs those stairs," he panted. "Where are all the little old ladies and pushchairs?"

"I don't know," Marit said. "But I hope they make it up somehow. Just look at that view."

They rounded the corner. The ancient basilica towered above them, its white marble walls and domed roof gleaming in the sunlight. Below, stretching out as far as the eye could see, was the city of Paris.

"Wow!" His burning muscles temporarily forgotten, Lars raised his camera and adjusted the focus.

Photographs of the panoramic view came first, and then he slowly made his way along the length of the overlook, snapping at least two dozen shots of the basilica from different angles. Finally, he swung around to capture Marit against the magnificent backdrop. She smiled—not the smile she offered the professional photographers she worked with regularly but the one reserved just for him. He lowered the camera, and closing the distance between them, he pressed a lingering kiss to her lips.

"Even with all that's happened over the last few days," he said, "I'm really glad we were able to experience Paris together."

"Yeah," she said. "Me too."

"I think maybe it's been good for Cole and Isabelle too."

Marit looked over his shoulder and smiled. "I think you're right."

Moments later, Cole appeared at Lars's side, his arm firmly around Isabelle.

"Well," Cole said, "you'll be pleased to know that Isabelle has figured out how the little old ladies and strollers get up here."

"How?" Lars asked.

Cole turned, drawing Isabelle with him so that Lars had a direct view of the people lined up on the other side of the road. As he watched, a rectangular object about the size of a lorry cab crested the hill.

"It's a funicular railway," Isabelle said. "And from what we can tell, it goes up and down the hill at fairly regular intervals."

In other words, they could have reached Sacré Cœur without climbing a single stair.

Lars glared at Cole. "Did you know about the funicular?"

Cole released Isabelle long enough to raise both hands. "Nope. And I'm as excited as you are to stop at a pâtisserie after we go down."

"On the funicular," Lars said firmly.

"Right." Isabelle offered him an encouraging smile. "No more stairs for us today."

"Except all the ones that lead into the basilica," Cole said.

Groaning, Lars reached for Marit's hand. "It's official. One way or another, Cole's going to kill me."

"Don't worry," Marit said. "We'll recruit Isabelle. Her self-defense skills are top-notch, and she's a really good teacher."

Isabelle laughed. "As long as you promise that I can be there when you first take Cole down, I'll teach you everything I know."

"You hear that, Cole?" Lars asked. "You're outnumbered."

With a grin, Cole led Isabelle toward the basilica's entrance. "In my line of work, I'm used to it."

OTHER BOOKS AND AUDIOBOOKS BY TRACI HUNTER ABRAMSON

Undercurrents Series

Undercurrents

Ripple Effect

The Deep End

Saint Squad Series

Freefall

Lockdown

Crossfire

Backlash

Smoke Screen

Code Word

Lock and Key

Drop Zone

Spotlight

Tripwire

Redemption

Covert Ops

Disconnect

Luke Steele Series

Hometown Vendetta

Royal Series

Royal Target

Royal Secrets

Royal Brides

Royal Heir

Royal Duty

Guardian Series

Failsafe

Safe House

Sanctuary

On the Run

In Harm's Way

Not Dead Yet

Unseen

Dream's Edge Series

*Dancing to Freedom**

An Unlikely Pair

*Broken Dreams**

Dreams of Gold

*The Best Mistake**

Worlds Collide

Falcon Point Series

Heirs of Falcon Point

The Danger with Diamonds

From an Unknown Sender

When Fashion Turns Deadly

Stand-Alones

Obsession

Proximity

*Twisted Fate**

*Entangled**

*Sinister Secrets**

Deep Cover

Mistaken Reality

Kept Secrets

Chances Are

Chance for Home

A Change of Fortune

The Fiction Kitchen Trio Cookbook

Jim and Katherine

* Novella

ABOUT THE AUTHOR

Traci Hunter Abramson, a former Central Intelligence Agency officer, was born in Arizona, where she lived until moving to Venezuela for a study-abroad program. After graduating from Brigham Young University, she worked for the CIA for six years until she resigned to raise her family. She credits the agency with giving her a wealth of ideas and skills needed to survive her children's teenage years.

Traci is a popular writing instructor and keynote speaker and enjoys sharing her knowledge with aspiring writers. She recently retired after spending twenty-six years coaching her local high school swim team and now spends a lot of time traveling, which she loves.

She has written more than forty best-selling novels and is a 2022 and 2023 Silver Falchion Award Mystery/Suspense finalist, 2022 Rone Award finalist, and eight-time Whitney Award winner, including Best Novel of the Year in both 2017 and 2019. She received the 2021 Swoony Award for Best Mystery/Suspense Romance.

She also loves hearing from her readers. If you would like to contact her, she can be reached through the following:

Website: www.traciabramson.com

Facebook page: facebook.com/tracihabramson

Facebook group: Traci's Friends

Bookbub: bookbub.com/authors/traci-hunter-abramson

X: @traciabramson

Instagram: instagram.com/traciabramson

OTHER BOOKS AND AUDIOBOOKS BY SIAN ANN BESSEY

Georgian Gentlemen Series

The Noble Smuggler

An Uncommon Earl

An Alleged Rogue

An Unfamiliar Duke

The Unassuming Curator

A Provincial Peer

Contemporary

Forgotten Notes

Cover of Darkness

Deception

You Came for Me

The Insider

The Gem Thief

Historical

Within the Dark Hills

One Last Spring

To Win a Lady's Heart

For Castle and Crown

The Heart of the Rebellion

The Call of the Sea

A Kingdom to Claim

Falcon Point Series

Heirs of Falcon Point

The Danger with Diamonds

From an Unknown Sender

When Fashion Turns Deadly

Kids on a Mission Series

Escape from Germany

Uprising in Samoa

Ambushed in Africa

Children's

A Family Is Forever

Teddy Bear, Blankie, and a Prayer

Anthologies and Booklets

The Perfect Gift

A Hopeful Christmas

No Strangers at Christmas

ABOUT THE AUTHOR

SIAN ANN BESSEY WAS BORN in Cambridge, England, and grew up on the island of Anglesey off the coast of North Wales. She left her homeland to attend university in the US, where she earned a bachelor's degree in communications, with a minor in English.

She began her writing career as a student, publishing several articles in magazines while still in college. Since then, she has published historical romance and romantic suspense novels, along with a variety of children's books. She is a *USA Today* best-selling author, a RONE Award runner-up, a Foreword Reviews Book of the Year finalist, and a Whitney Award finalist.

Sian and her husband, Kent, are the parents of five children and the grandparents of four beautiful girls and two handsome boys. They currently live in southeast Idaho, and although Sian doesn't have the opportunity to speak Welsh very often anymore, *Llanfairpwllgwyngyllgogerychwyrndrobwllllantysiliogogogoch* still rolls off her tongue.

Traveling, reading, cooking, and being with her grandchildren are some of Sian's favorite activities. She also loves hearing from her readers. If you would like to contact her, she can be reached through her website at www.sianannbessey.com. You can also follow her on social media. Find the links on her website.